raised forever

JESUS' RESURRECTION AND OURS

Rory Shiner

Guidebooks for Life

Bible-based essentials
for your Christian journey

Raised Forever is part of a series of straightforward,
practical Christian books from Matthias Media which
deal with the important nuts-and-bolts topics that
Christians need to know about as we walk each day with
our Master.

Some Christian books are all theory and no practical
application; others are all stories and tips with no
substance. The Guidebooks for Life aim to achieve a
vital balance—that is, to dig into the Bible and discover
what God is telling us there, as well as applying that
truth to our daily Christian lives.

For up-to-date information about the latest
Guidebooks for Life, visit our website:
www.matthiasmedia.com/gfl

Guidebooks for Life

raised forever

JESUS' RESURRECTION AND OURS

Rory Shiner

matthiasmedia

Raised Forever
© Matthias Media 2014

Matthias Media
(St Matthias Press Ltd ACN 067 558 365)
Email: info@matthiasmedia.com.au
Internet: www.matthiasmedia.com.au
Please visit our website for current postal and telephone contact information.

Matthias Media (USA)
Email: sales@matthiasmedia.com
Internet: www.matthiasmedia.com
Please visit our website for current postal and telephone contact information.

ISBN 978 1 922206 62 6

Cover design and typesetting by Lankshear Design.

CONTENTS

For my cousins,
Paul Neil Brown (1976-1980)
and Cameron Marshall Harris (1974-2011).

Even such is time, which takes in trust
Our youth, our joys, and all we have,
And pays us but with age and dust,
Who in the dark and silent grave
When we have wandered all our ways
Shuts up the story of our days,
And from which earth, and grave, and dust
The Lord will raise me up, I trust.

—Sir Walter Raleigh, 1618
(on the night before he was executed)

INTRODUCTION

You're in a garden. It's early in the morning. And it's still dark.

You see a young woman come into the garden (well, garden/graveyard) to pay her respects at the grave of a loved one. Graveyards aren't convivial places at the best of times, but on this morning the woman finds something deeply disturbing. Her friend's grave has been tampered with. The stone that blocked off the entrance to the tomb has been removed. Someone, it seems, has been in there before she arrived. Who knows, maybe that person is still here somewhere, hiding behind one of the other tombs? Creepy.

What would you be thinking? Someone has been here before. And they wanted to get into the grave. But why? Did they want to do something with (or to) the body? Why would someone want a dead body? Why so early in the morning? And why that particular dead body?

So she runs back to where her friends are staying.

"They've taken the body!", she tells them. "They've taken the body out of the tomb, and I don't know where they have put him." (To whom the 'they' in that sentence refers is unclear to everyone, including her.)

Two men start running toward the garden. The younger one gets there first, but he doesn't go in. He looks in from the outside, and sees exactly what the woman had said—that there is no body inside. He can see from the entrance the strips of linen with which the body had been wrapped.

The older man arrives shortly after, but rather than stopping at the entrance, he runs straight in.

And he sees the same thing—an empty tomb. And he notices the linen has not just been left behind in a mess, but that the head-dress is separate from the linen that was around the body.

What sense do you make of a scene like that? The woman is right. The body is not there. Clearly someone has taken it. That's the woman's conclusion. This happened in about the year 33 AD, but people back then didn't jump to supernatural conclusions willy-nilly. None of them see the empty tomb and think, "Miracle!" On the contrary, they, like us, conclude: if a dead body is not where you left it, a living person has done something to it. Dead bodies aren't the subjects of verbs, but their objects. As a rule, they don't *do* anything (except decompose). They can only have things done to them.

But that raises questions. Why has someone taken this body? And, if you are stealing a body for who knows what purposes, why strip the linen off first? How exactly does it make your job easy to ensure the body is naked prior to departure?

> Jerusalem citizen: Hi Jerry, you're up early. What are you doing?
>
> Jerry the Grave Robber: Oh, nothing really. Just going for a walk. Lovely morning.
>
> Jerusalem citizen: Jerry, is that a dead naked body you've got there?
>
> Jerry: Um...

Furthermore, if you're stealing a dead body early on a Sunday morning, my guess is that you feel a little, well, sheepish about the whole exercise. Like you're doing something a bit out of the ordinary—something on which society might frown. Something you wouldn't tell your mum about. So, if you're *that* guy (the 'who cares what mum and society thinks I'm getting me a dead naked body' guy), how likely is it that you're also a bit of a neat-freak? That you're someone who has been raised to leave places neater than you found them so that you neatly fold and separate the grave clothes before you leave?

> Grave robber 1: We've got the body. Let's go!
>
> Grave robber 2: Michael! We can't just leave the place like this. This is disgusting! The least we can do is spend a few minutes cleaning up. Here, help me fold this linen.

Meanwhile, the woman is out in the garden crying. Probably not standard-issue 'someone I love is dead' tears, but a rather more complex and desperate stream of 'my friend is dead and something really weird and possibly creepy has happened to his body' tears.

A man comes up to her and asks her, "Why are you weeping? Whom are you seeking?"

She thinks he's the gardener and so she says, "Sir, if you have carried him away, tell me where you have laid him, and I will take him away".

And the gardener says to her, "Mary".

And she exclaims, "*Rabboni!*", which means, "my teacher".

This, of course, is an account of the resurrection (or, if you prefer, *alleged* resurrection) of a Jewish Rabbi from the first century called Yeshua Ben Joseph, who is known to us as Jesus. It is from the Gospel of John. Three days earlier, Jesus had been crucified and laid in a tomb. And according to John, and to the early Christian witness in general, somewhere in the early hours of the first day of the week, on a day we call Sunday, in a month we call April, the tomb was found empty, and followers of Jesus soon after began reporting that they had seen him alive.

It's a remarkable account, full of eyewitness-like details: the time of day, how the grave clothes were arranged, the names of the people involved and the order in which they arrived. For all sorts of reasons, it's a report of events we are supposed to infer actually happened, in our world, and at a particular time and place. (Whether they did in fact happen or not we shall consider later in chapter 3. The point is that John wants to give the impression these things happened. He's either writing history, or trying to give the impression of writing history. He's not writing myth.)

This is a book about the resurrection.

It's not a book (just) about the resurrection of Jesus. There are plenty of those from both sceptics and believers alike. Neither is it a book (just) about what happens when we die. Again, there are plenty of books about what happens when we die and how the world may or may not end.

This book is about what Paul was talking about when he preached to the Athenians about "Jesus and *the* resurrection" (Acts 17:18). It is about what Peter and John were talking about when they were preaching to the people of Jerusalem, "proclaiming *in Jesus* the resurrection from the dead" (Acts 4:2). It is about what the Apostles' Creed means when it mentions *both* the resurrection of Jesus ("on the third day he rose again from the dead") and the resurrection of us all ("I believe in the resurrection of the body"). That is, it is a book about what happened to Jesus, what will happen to us, and *how those two things connect.*

Now of course we must ask the 'did it happen' question. As John Updike says in his poem on the resurrection of Jesus:

> Let us not mock God with metaphor...
> making of the event a parable...
> let us walk through the door.[1]

The resurrection can't mean what it means (either for Jesus or for us) if it didn't actually happen. Not everything is like that. Some things (like Aesop's Fables or some of Jesus' own parables) can mean what they mean perfectly well apart from actually happening. But the resurrection of Jesus isn't one of those things, for reasons we shall explore. We shall be walking through that door—the door of history—gladly and necessarily.

But the burden of this book is not to prove that Jesus' resurrection happened. Why not? Because my observation is that most Christians have precisely no trouble accepting Jesus rose from the dead. This is not necessarily because we've all spent a lot of time surveying the data, but simply because we assume that believing in Jesus' resurrection is part of the Christian package. (And anyway, if that is your particular itch, there are plenty of good books written to scratch exactly there.)[2] However, my observation is also that most Christians have precisely A Lot Of Trouble connecting what happened to Jesus with what will happen to us and to our world.

Let me put it this way: once you've 'proved' the resurrection of Jesus, what exactly have you proved? That

---

1   J Updike, 'Seven Stanzas at Easter', in *Telephone Poles and other Poems*, Knopf, New York, 1963, pp. 72-3.

2   I'll refer to several of these books in chapter 3.

Jesus is God? That he is the Son of God? That the cross worked? That there's an afterlife? That a supernatural worldview is valid and evidence-based?

Actually, none of those are really where the New Testament goes when it talks about what the resurrection of Jesus means. But it goes *somewhere*. It has things—profound things—to say about what the resurrection of Jesus means. And, just as it is perfectly reasonable to expect a well-instructed Christian to be able to articulate what the cross achieved for us, I think it's also perfectly reasonable for a well-instructed Christian to be able to articulate what the resurrection of Jesus means for us. That's the purpose of this book.

So, here's how we'll proceed. Let's start where most encounters with the resurrection start—with preaching. First, we'll visit Athens and listen in as Paul proclaims the resurrection to sophisticated and sceptical pagans. Then, in chapter 2, let's go to Jerusalem and listen in on Peter as he proclaimed the resurrection to a very different crowd: a group of deeply religious Jews at Pentecost. Then, in chapter 3, we return to that garden to ask the 'what happened' question, the 'how could you know' question, and the 'how far can the evidence really get you' question.

Then, in chapters 4 through to 7, we will be thinking deeply about the connections between what happened in that garden, what will happen to our bodies and to our world, and what difference it makes now.

I would be surprised if there weren't some surprises in store for you. There certainly were for me. I've had to re-think the way I use the word 'heaven', clarify my beliefs about where those who've died as Christians are now, and re-evaluate my understanding of the true nature of Christian hope. It's sometimes been disconcerting, but almost always thrilling, as I've discovered the Christian hope to be deeper, richer and more compelling than I ever did before. I hope the same thing happens for you.

But back to the garden. John has us focused on Mary alone. We know from the other Gospels that there were other women there. John knows it too—note the plural in John 20:2 when Mary says, "They have taken the Lord out of the tomb and *we* do not know where they have laid him". John knows there were other women with Mary. And yet he wants us to have an image in our minds: the image of a man and a woman together in a garden. Why?

Man. Woman. Garden. Ring any bells? When is the last time in the Bible you saw a man and a woman in a garden?

Maybe John wants us to see that now, on this morning, in this garden, the new creation has begun.[3]

---

3   An insight suggested to me by Tom Wright's comments on page 146 of *John for Everyone* (SPCK, London, 2002).

Chapter 1

THE STRANGE HOPE— RESURRECTION AMONG THE SCEPTICS

New cities, fresh eyes

I was 21 when I first visited London, having grown up in Australia. I stayed for three months overall, and most of those days have now been forgotten, amalgamated with subsequent trips or merged into a vague montage of Londonness in my mind.

But not the first day. Now, nearly 20 years later, I could take you almost minute by minute through all I noticed on that first day: the yellow signage at Heathrow, the Hasidic Jewish man who walked past me near the luggage carrousel, the bracing four-degree-Celsius October morning, the smell of cigarette smoke and general dampness as I walked out of the airport, the way the roof was surprisingly low on the Piccadilly line train to Hammersmith, and the milky cup of tea in the thick-rimmed mug that my host offered me on arrival. On that day, new to the city and with my eyes wide open, I noticed everything.

It's a common experience for visitors to a new city. For those first 24 hours, everything feels like it's suddenly being broadcast in high definition. Your senses kick into overdrive and everything looks, smells and sounds different, bigger and more vivid. It's pretty fantastic.

And then it stops. Surprisingly quickly, what was once fascinating in the new city becomes unremarkable, and you just can't see it any more.

The Christian hope

In this book, I want to tell a story—the story of how Christians came to their distinctive hope for the future, a hope they call 'resurrection'. And our story begins with a man who, like me on that October day, was a stranger in a new city, and who, as is the way, had his senses kicked into overdrive as he saw things the locals didn't see. The man was Paul, the city was Athens, and what he noticed was the idols.

Athens

Athens was a city whose fame went before it. It was and is the city of Socrates, Plato and Aristotle; a city whose name evoked hushed tones as one recalled the intellectual and artistic achievements with which its citizens were credited. Although its heyday was several centuries earlier, Athens still basked in the afterglow of its greatness. It remained one of the great intellectual centres of the Roman world, a great—maybe *the* great—university town. If anyone wanted to change the world, to go culturally up-stream, to reach the elites, then Athens would be the place to start.

However, Paul (who is perhaps *less* strategic at this point than we give him credit for) appears to have had no plans for mission in the great city. Rather, having been suddenly and unexpectedly sent out from Berea (Acts 17:14-15), he was in Athens as a mere travel contingency, waiting there for Timothy and Silas to arrive (v. 16).

What does a visitor notice in Athens? The architecture? The sculpture? The sense of nobility and high vision for human flourishing? What Paul noticed is surprising: the city was full of idols.

At least, it's a surprise to me. You see, I don't think Paul would have been shocked in quite the way that an innocent youth from a conservative rural family might be shocked at his discoveries in a major city. Paul was not easily shocked. Though from a minority religious group (the Jews), he was also a man of the world, educated in the best of Greek culture. A man as well-travelled as Paul would know that the Gentiles went for idolatry in a pretty big way. The town he had just left (Berea) would have had idols in it, and the next town, Corinth, was no slouch when it came to idols either.

The point is that Paul had seen plenty of idols in his time. And yet here in Athens "his spirit was provoked within him" (Acts 17:16) in some more-than-usual way. Why? It could be the *quantity* of idols—that Athens just had a greater idols-per-square-capita ratio than anywhere he'd been before, and the words Luke (the author of Acts) uses here might suggest that.[4] It could be the *quality* of the Athenians' piety—something other ancient visitors also noticed.[5] However, it could be that part of Paul's reaction came not so much from how many idols there were, or how into them the Athenians were, but from *who* had the idols. The Athenians! You rational Athenians? Of all people!? Oh my.

A city full of idols

Paul notices the idols and, more than that, he finds them distressing. He responds, however, not by attacking their productions, but by attacking their reason. He does not smash their idols down, but he begins to chip away at the reasoning that made the idols possible.

---

4   D Peterson, *The Acts of the Apostles*, Apollos, Grand Rapids, 2009, p. 488.
5   FF Bruce, *The Book of Acts*, Eerdmans, Grand Rapids, 1988, p. 335, footnote 54.

And it doesn't go that well. A group of Epicurean and Stoic philosophers eventually begin to debate with him in the marketplace. The Epicureans were sceptical about the gods having a role in everyday life, and were critical of popular religion and its tendency to locate the gods in idols and temples. They lived a kind of practical atheism. The Stoics believed in the divine 'Logos': in reason being grounded in the divine Reason. And they believed that all humans were descended from a single ancestor.[6] Which is to say, Paul's message should have gotten a bit of traction with these guys. (If what he says next is anything like what he was saying in the marketplace, it seems almost tailor-made for this crowd.) But the reaction seems to be evenly divided between two pretty discouraging responses:

> ...And some said, "What does this babbler wish to say?" Others said, "He seems to be a preacher of foreign divinities"—because he was preaching Jesus and the resurrection. (Acts 17:18)

On the first reaction (the "What does this babbler wish to say?" reaction), maybe Paul had a regional accent, and, together with the noisy circumstances of the marketplace, it was probably hard to understand him. (The massive curiosity of Greek culture for almost every area of life didn't seem to have extended much into linguistics— those who did not speak their language were literally

---

6   Peterson, *Acts*, p. 490.

'babblers' or 'nonsense-speakers', from where we get the word 'barbarians'.)

The second objection is a bit more baffling. Given that Paul was a monotheist of the strict Jewish variety, and given that he was moved to speak because Athens had far too many gods, the idea that he was advocating *more* foreign gods is ironic. Why did they think that? To solve this mystery, you have to imagine yourself in that noisy marketplace, hearing this man speaking and repeating, again and again, two words: *Iesous* and *Anastasis*. *Iesous* sounds like a boy's name and *Anastasis* sounds like a girl's name. And if that's as much as you can make out, you end up concluding that, like Osiris and Isis, he is advocating new male and female gods: the male god *Iesous* and his consort *Anastasis*.

However, as you know, Paul was not talking about two gods or even two people. He was talking about a man called Jesus (*Iesous*) and a thing called resurrection (*Anastasis*). (Notice, by the way, that he's not talking about Jesus and *his* resurrection, but Jesus and *the* resurrection. Is that what you'd speak about if you had an unexpected chance to preach the gospel? Jesus and *the* resurrection of the dead? Me neither.)

Mars Hill

Paul's experience in the marketplace wasn't great, but neither was it a total write-off. Paul attracted enough attention to be invited up to the Areopagus—to Mars Hill, the very place where the greatest philosophers of Athens expounded their noblest ideas—to give a fuller account of his strange ideas about *Iesous* and *Anastasis*. (If you're wondering how people were able to just drop everything to go listen to a lecture, Luke explains it in verse 21: "Now all the Athenians and the foreigners who lived there would spend their time in nothing except telling or hearing something new". Nice work if you can get it.)

Now, as he hits the speech proper, remember: Paul is there to give account of his strange ideas regarding Jesus and the resurrection. At several points in the speech (and consequently in this chapter), it might feel like Paul has wandered some way off the reservation. But he's smarter than that. Go with him, and see how he brings it all to bear on our topic.

Paul begins his address with these words: "Men of Athens, I perceive that in every way you are very religious" (Acts 17:22). Why does he start the speech like that? It could be that the speaker is simply complimenting his audience. In the same way an out-of-town speaker might comment favourably on the food (Singapore), the architecture (Paris) or the harbour (Sydney), it could be that Paul is simply commending their sincere piety.

It could be that he is creating common ground with his audience. He observes that they both—audience and speaker—have a declared interest in knowing God, and it is on that shared matter of concern that he wishes to address them. Certainly the speech as a whole contains bold and breathtaking elements of bridge-building with pagans, and so an appeal here to common ground would be by no means out of place.

But let me try an alternative out on you. Paul, you see, found the idols distressing, not impressive (v. 16). And in verse 22 he uses the word *deisidaimonesterous*, which the ESV has translated as 'religious' but which could also be translated as 'credulous' or 'superstitious'.[7] And given the way Paul's speech proceeds, I wonder if the force of it is that he's saying to *them*—to the rational, logic-loving Athenians—sympathetically but critically, "I'm surprised to discover that for all your rationalism, you're actually rather religious". To get the tone right, imagine the way you'd respond if you discovered your nanna was mad keen on late 1990s gangster hip-hop: "*You*, Nanna? *You're* into hip hop?" Notice the way your intonation went up at the end? Read Paul's sentence like that. "*You* guys? You, of all people, are *religious*?'

And with that, Paul launches into his standard Jewish critique of idolatry. Idolatry is the symptom of a profound brokenness in our understanding of God. Even if it starts out with the best intentions as a worship strategy, idolatry always ends up as a containment policy, and ultimately as a distortion of God. "We ought not to think", says Paul, "that the divine being is like gold or silver or stone, an image formed by the art and imagination of man" (17:29).

---

7   Danker (ed.), *A Greek–English Lexicon of the New Testament and Other Early Christian Literature* (BDAG), 3rd edn, University of Chicago Press, Chicago, 2000 [1957], p. 216.

Almost all religions in Paul's day had idols, temples and sacrifices. They were in many ways the trifecta of any self-respecting religion. They were religion's sacred cows (and yes, I realize how messed up that metaphor is in this context). In this speech, Paul goes after all three of them.

Humans should not worship idols. God made us, and made us to bear his image (Gen 1:27). We should not worship the images of our own creation.

Neither should we think of God as living in temples. If your god can live in a temple, your god is too small. Paul's own people had an inner tension at this point. They had a temple, sure. And in some sense God's presence was there. But at the very founding of their first temple, their great king Solomon asked, "Will God indeed dwell on the earth? Behold, heaven and the highest heaven cannot contain you; how much less this house that I have built!" (1 Kgs 8:27). The prophets never stopped reminding them of this fact: God graced the temple of Israel with his presence, but he was never contained there. The truth is, we don't make a home for God; God has, in this creation, made a home for us.

We don't get to house God, and neither do we sacrifice to God. We do not feed God, bringing him his food as if he were our pet dog, hungry and depending on us. It is he who gives us our food, our life, our breath, and everything else (Acts 17:25). Again, Israel experienced a tension here. Sacrifice was part of their religion, and yet again and again they were reminded that their sacrifices did not meet a need in God. So in Psalm 50:

"I will not accept a bull from your house
  or goats from your folds.
For every beast of the forest is mine,
  the cattle on a thousand hills.
I know all the birds of the hills,
  and all that moves in the field is mine." (Ps 50:9-11)

If God created all things, they are his. He may give them to us, but we can't *really* give them to him.

In short: we don't make images of God; God has placed his image on us. We don't make homes for God; God made a home for us. And we don't provide for God; God provides for us. Get these things the wrong way around and pretty soon you can't think coherently about God, let alone worship God at all.

Humans, you see, are worshipping creatures, and when we try and suppress this part of our nature, it's like trying to hold a balloon under a swimming pool—the worship instinct just keeps insisting it comes to the surface. But it comes up to the surface in weird forms. As GK Chesterton said, when we cease to worship the true and living God then instead of worshipping nothing, we find ourselves worshipping anything. If there is a God-shaped hole in every human heart, it is not an empty hole. It is crammed full of things that awkwardly and imperfectly fill the available space.

There is a famous parody of idolatry in the Old Testament when the prophet Isaiah asks the simple question, "Where do idols come from?" (Isa 44:9-20). Because, the truth be told, they don't just fall out of heaven. In reality, a guy walks into a forest and cuts down a tree. He uses half the wood to make a fire. He gets hungry or cold, and so he burns the wood and cooks his food on the fire, saying, "Ah, this is good. I am warm."

With the other half of his piece of wood, he makes a god. He chips away, shaping it and forming it with his knife and his axe. Sometimes he's up close doing the detailed work; other times he stands back, index finger pressed against his lips, leaning his head to one side and then to the other, seeing that he has the shape and proportions just right. He fusses and thinks and chips and shapes and forms. And then (the fatal misstep) he bows down to it and says, "Save me, you are my god".

And Isaiah says, "Mate! You *made* that! *You* made it! Like, half an hour ago. Have you forgotten?"

If anything, the idol should bow down to *you* and say, "Thank you for my existence". You could place it in an art gallery and write underneath: Eric Made This. But whatever you do, don't bow down to it. If it has any function at all, it is surely to bring you glory; don't you bring it glory. It owes you everything; you owe it nothing.

The Jewish people were forbidden from making images, not because no image of God was possible, but because God had already put an image of himself in the creation—namely, us humans. From the Jewish point of view, the image-bearers of God worshipping images they had made was so ironic that it risked opening up an irony vortex in the fabric of the universe so ironic that it could suck all lesser ironies into itself. Humans are not supposed to worship images of God; they *are* the image of God. Idol worship makes absolutely no sense.

God has left his image in the universe. The whole of creation is supposed to be able to look at us and see that we bear the imprint of God. The cosmos is supposed to learn its most basic theological lesson from observing humanity. If nature had a catechism, and the question was, "What is God like?", the creation should be able affirm that God is (and I can't believe I'm going to say this out loud, but the Bible requires it) *like us*.

Modern idolatry

Now, you might hear all that and say, "Well, there's an obvious gap here. Modernity has succeeded where Athens failed. We have achieved the dream: rationalism without religion, science without superstition, progress without piety." Would a modern Paul find himself walking around New York or London or Melbourne and be struck by how religious those cities are?

Well, it depends on how you understand idolatry.

There is a literal sense to idolatry in the Bible. The people of God were forbidden from worshipping literal idols—either images of the true God or idols of false gods. And Paul in Athens certainly doesn't lose sight of this—he quite specifically calls the Athenians on their images "formed by the art and imagination of man" (Acts 17:29). When I was being taught to read the Bible, I was told, "When the plain sense makes sense, seek no other sense". And the plain sense of the word 'idolatry' is, in the majority of cases, 'worshipping idols'. John warns his Christian readers, "Little children, keep yourselves from idols" (1 John 5:21). And I'm pretty sure he means idols.

However, the Bible does make a crucial step in its teaching on idolatry. Paul is (twice!) able to talk about covetousness or greed and name that as a form of idolatry (Eph 5:5, Col 3:5). Paul is also able to talk about an obsession with orthodox religious practice becoming a god in place of the true God (Phil 3:19). And Jesus puts money and God before his follows, not as a choice between secularity and religion but as a choice between two religions. Notice Jesus' language: "No-one can *serve* two masters, for either he will hate the one and love the other, or he will be *devoted* to the one and despise the other. You cannot *serve* God and money" (Matt 6:24).

The point? Simply that if idolatry is not less that the worship of images, it certainly includes more than that. Indeed, according to Jesus and to Paul, whenever a human heart offers its loyalty and devotion to created things rather than the Creator, you are looking at a form of idolatry. Just so you can spot it in the wild, this form of idolatry is *when things that are less than God take the place of God in our lives.*

That's what happened literally to our friend in the forest in Isaiah's story, isn't it? He goes into the forest, makes something, and then says to that thing (which is less than God, and in fact even less than him), "Be my god". And that's the kind of thing Paul has in mind, surely, when he addresses the greedy, covetous person for whom material possessions have become that which they obsess over, fight for and sacrifice to. And that's what Jesus has in mind, surely, when he casts God and money as two gods, in competition for our devotion and service.

And if idolatry is when things that are smaller than God become bigger than God, to the exclusion of God, then isn't that what is happening in Western cities all the time? Isn't that what is happening when our careers, our jobs and our 'productions' become things that control us instead of things that we control? Isn't that what you see in materialism, when people are willing to sacrifice all that is good and all that contributes to human flourishing in order to possess more and more?

Isn't that what you see in the nation state? Consider the rivers of blood that flowed in the 20th century for the sake of 'the nation'. Consider the songs and flags and memorials and sacred spaces that war and nationalism have made a part of the rhythms and practices of modern Western cities. (Imagine, for example, taking a foreign visitor to an Australian Anzac Day dawn service and then trying to persuade them over lunch that Australia isn't very religious.)

Isn't that what you see in modern relationships? Have you noticed the way the language of devotion, service, meaning and loyalty have gathered like pins to a magnet around romantic relationships? Notice, as one of a million possible examples, the words of the Simon and Garfunkel classic, 'Kathy's Song':

So you see I have come to doubt,
All that I once held as true.

I stand alone without belief.
The only truth I know is you.[8]

See what they did there? All the weight of human longing and religious impulse, the weight of worship, is about to land on poor Kathy's shoulders. And no human shoulders were made to bear that sort of weight.

I think Paul would see our pop songs, our war memorials, our flags, our devotion to possessions and positions, and he would say to us, "Do you know what? For all your secularity, I think you're still very religious".

God

"The God who made the world and everything in
it, being Lord of heaven and earth, does not live in
temples made by man." (Acts 17:24)

If you declare your belief in God to an atheist, there is a good chance they will reply by asking, "Which one?" The truth is, there are thousands of gods that none of us believes in. Mars, Aphrodite and the Flying Spaghetti Monster have no temples and receive no prayers from us. As the joke goes, when it comes to unbelief, atheists beat Christians by just one god.

At one level, the joke works. Indeed, it can be a healthy little reminder to Christians that the Bible was written in

---

8   P Simon, 'Kathy's Song', from the album *Sounds of Silence*, Columbia
    Records, New York, 1965.

a time in which the word 'god' often did not have an agreed referent, and you had to qualify your god as 'the God of Abraham, Isaac and Jacob' or 'the God who raised Jesus Christ from the dead'. It is the truth Robert Jenson points to in his wonderful theological affirmation: "God is whoever raised Jesus from the dead, having before raised Israel from Egypt".[9]

But at another level the joke masks a significant category error, a conflation of two very different concepts. 'The gods' were divine beings, allegedly inhabiting the universe. 'God', on the other hand, refers to the transcendent source of all being, someone outside the cosmos. 'The gods' had births and sometimes even deaths. They played and fought and loved and lost. For their believers, they were part of the inventory of 'stuff that exists', along with coffee tables and banjos and electric blankets. 'God', on the other hand, is outside of creation. He is not on the list of stuff within it. This might sound like special pleading on the part of Christians. It's not. It is an unremarkable distinction that, according to David Bentley Hart, goes back in the Greek tradition at least as far as Xenophanes, and one that is readily understood in Islam, Judaism, forms of Hinduism, and Deism.[10] Indeed, when Paul wants to make this exact point, he quotes not from

9   RW Jenson, *Systematic Theology*, vol. 1, *The Triune God*, OUP, Oxford, 1997, p. 63.
10   DB Hart, 'God, gods, and fairies', *First Things*, June-July 2013, available online (viewed 10 September 2013): http://firstthings.com/article/2013/06/god-gods-and-fairies

the Old Testament, but from the Cretan philosopher Epimenides, who says (originally of Zeus), "For in him we live and move and have our being" (Acts 17:28).[11]

And so, belief in God—in this God, in the God who is the ground and source of all being—might not be so easily dismissed as Hermes, Mars and the gang. Indeed, the way in which you would assess the existence of 'the gods', if you could be bothered, would be very different from the way in which you would assess the existence of God.

Consider Shakespeare's play *Hamlet*.[12] Shakespeare creates a world populated with characters: Ophelia, Claudius, Horatio and Hamlet himself. And the gods are like that: characters who inhabit our world.

But when Christians speak of God, he is not a character in our world. He is not present in the drama as a character is present in *Hamlet*. No, God's relationship to our world is like Shakespeare's relationship to *Hamlet*. On the one hand, Shakespeare is nowhere present in *Hamlet*. An exhaustive search through each scene of the play will reveal a Shakespeare-free world. He is simply not there. And yet on the other hand, as we know, Shakespeare is the ground and source of all being in the play, the one through whom they all live and move and have their being.

---

11 J Dickson, 'Some atheist jokes deserve to be laughed at', ABC, Ultimo, 8 July 2013 (viewed 19 December 2013): http://abc.net.au/religion/articles/2013/07/08/3798272.htm

12 The analogy that follows was first suggested to me by CS Lewis in his essay 'The Seeing Eye'. See *The Seeing Eye and other Selected Essays from Christian Reflections*, ed. W Hooper, Ballantine Books, New York, 1967, p. 167.

That (or something very like it) is the understanding of God with which Paul is operating in this speech to the Athenians. It is a concept of God he presents in good faith, assuming they can grasp it—even to the point of rallying some theology-of-Zeus in support.[13] Although Paul is a Jewish thinker, his ideas ought to have found a ready reception in some of the Stoics or Epicureans to whom they were addressed.

History

But as Paul's talk draws to a close, he makes another claim—one that is based neither in metaphysics nor in a doctrine of God and creation. Paul's claim is based in history. To this classical view of God, he introduces a new way of approaching the issue. To a talk that's been largely about ideas, he now adds something that is not conceptual, but historical. He has some *news*:

> "The times of ignorance God overlooked, but now he commands all people everywhere to repent, because he has fixed a day on which he will judge the world in righteousness by a man whom he has appointed; and of this he has given assurance to all by raising him from the dead." (Acts 17:30-31)

Notice all the time references: there was the time of ignorance, but *now* God commands all people to repent,

---

13 J Dickson, 'Atheist jokes'.

because in the future a day has been fixed for judgement, and the man who will do the judging has already been appointed. Something has happened. Paul can discuss ideas with the best of them, but he also has news to declare. He has a gospel.

And his gospel (that is, his news, his big news) is that God has set a day when he will judge the world with justice (v. 31). Paul comes with the news that God will one day draw the sorry drama of human history to a close, that he will vindicate the oppressed, and bring the oppressor to justice. Paul declares that God will expel sin and evil from the drama, that he will bring comfort to the afflicted, hope to the lost, and justice to everyone. He declares that God will judge the living and the dead. In this part of the news, Paul is simply reiterating what Isaiah or Daniel or any number of Old Testament prophets would have said and did say. "Let the heavens be glad, and let the earth rejoice", says the psalmist, "...for he comes to judge the earth. He will judge the world in righteousness, and the peoples in his faithfulness" (Ps 96:11, 13).

But Paul's news goes one step further. To the chorus of Old Testament witnesses to the coming judgement of God, to the claim that 'God will judge the world in righteousness', Paul adds a new song. Not only will God come with justice, but he has now taken the step of appointing his judge. And how was this judge appointed? Well, "by raising him from the dead" of course.

What does the resurrection of Jesus mean? Well, in the first instance, it means that Jesus is the judge of the living and the dead. We will be judged. (That's why we are raised, by the way. Remember how, back in the marketplace, Paul was talking about Jesus and *the* resurrection? He was talking about *our* resurrection— that one day we will stand before God in our bodies to receive his judgement.) And Jesus, raised ahead of time, has been appointed by God to be our judge. That was the heart of Paul's gospel on that day. That's why he doesn't end the speech by asking the Athenians to 'invite Jesus into their hearts', but rather to prepare to meet him on his throne.

Think back to Shakespeare. The author is not a character in the play, and it is entirely at Shakespeare's prerogative to create a world entirely independent of him. But Shakespeare could *choose* to write himself into the play. Shakespeare could choose to reveal himself to the players. And in the incarnation and the resurrection of Jesus, the author of creation has played his hand. The author has told the players what the final chapter involves. And, it turns out, we are not in a tragedy, or a comedy, or a romance (though there are elements of all three). We are in a vindication play. It's one where a lost and rebellious world is judged and renewed by its creator. And the story is nearing its very last scene. The judge is appointed and ready. God gave this assurance to all by raising him from the dead. We now know what the last scene will look like.

Conclusion

It's hard to imagine a better speech from a Christian preaching to the members of the Areopagus. It's sophisticated. It's learned. He quotes their poets and their philosophers. And yet it's a long way from a raging success. Many scoff, some want to hear more, and a few believe (Acts 17:32-34). It's hardly a Billy Graham moment.

Where did Paul hit the hard travelling in his argument? Verse 32: "Now when they heard of the resurrection of the dead, some mocked". That seems to be the catch. And the truth is that as much as Paul goes out of his way to address them in words and language and categories they will understand, the meaning of the resurrection is inescapably embedded in the story of Israel. Paul is an impressive model of sympathetic, culturally engaged, intelligent evangelism. And he manages to give the whole speech without explicitly quoting the Bible. However, the story of Israel is only just under the surface. And in those last words—"he has given assurance to all by raising him from the dead"—it sticks up over the surface. Paul has taken them a long way—a very long way—but ultimately the logic of resurrection is, as I shall argue in the next chapter, embedded in the logic of Israel's own story. And so, in the next chapter, we will consider the story of the resurrection as the fulfilment of Israel's story—which is what Peter, on the day of Pentecost, says it is.

But before we leave the sceptics, consider what Paul has put before them and before us. Paul does not give proof *for* the resurrection; for him, the resurrection *is* proof—proof of the coming justice of God. He argues *from* the resurrection, not *for* it.[14] Under those circumstances, what was it that led those few to believe?

Maybe Paul's concept of God made sense to them. After all, he was able to quote what a Greek poet had said about Zeus as evidence for what he (Paul) believed about God. Maybe there is something deep within us that remembers our high calling as image-bearers, such that when someone points out to us the absurdity of idolatry, we intuitively think, "Yeah, this is nuts!"

Maybe Paul's concept of the coming judgement of God made sense. From the ancient Egyptians to the modern Kantians, Paul's audience wouldn't be the first or only people outside of Christianity who are attracted to the moral power and explanatory possibilities that come from postulating a final day of reckoning.[15]

Winston Churchill reportedly once said that democracy is the worst system of government, except for every other system of government. Maybe at one level believing in the resurrection of one man's body in history, and in the resurrection of all of our bodies in the future, is… well, nuts. Maybe it's the worst (= least likely, most counter-intuitive) of all the possible scenarios for the end of the world and the life of the world to come. But maybe, just maybe, embedded

---

14 Whether and to what extent we can arrive at proof *for* the resurrection is a question we will consider in chapter 3.

15 Immanuel Kant (1724-1804) was a philosopher who, among other things, believed in a day of judgement from God not on the basis of the Bible but as a kind of logical necessity.

within resurrection belief is a surprising power to account for some of our deepest intuitions as humans: that death is, in some strange sense, an enemy; that human life is, in some irreducible sense, embodied life; that someone really ought to call sin and evil to account; that this world is not the best of all possible worlds. Maybe, having explored the other possibilities, we sceptical people might come back to the hope of the resurrection because (to use CS Lewis's language), like the sun, it sheds light on everything else.

Chapter 2

THE DISTANT HOPE—
RESURRECTION AND THE
STORY OF ISRAEL

IN ATHENS, PAUL PROCLAIMED the resurrection and a few people believed (Acts 17:34). By no means a total waste of time, but neither was it an unmitigated success. Like the modern, secular West, Athens was not a place with much low-hanging fruit for the evangelist to harvest. Athens was a tough gig. Surely this stuff would get a better hearing in a place like Jerusalem—good old end-times obsessed, religiously nutty, politically volatile, resurrection-oriented Jerusalem. And the stats seem to confirm it did: at the end of Peter's speech in Jerusalem on the topic of the resurrection, about 3,000 people were added to their number (Acts 2:41). If we put the number of people responding at the end of Paul's speech at a generous 20, it would seem that Peter's speech was about 15,000% more effective. Not bad. Not bad at all.

However, it is extremely unlikely that Luke meant us to run the odds and conclude that we should preach more like Peter and less like Paul—Acts being a book less about 'How To Make Your Church Grow Big' and more about 'How To Still Sing Songs Whilst In Prison for Jesus'. And Peter's 'success' on that day surely had an awful lot to do with the kind of mental furniture already in the minds of his Old-Testament-soaked audience.

And that is true—*but not in the way many of us imagine*. It's true that Peter's Jerusalem audience were Old-Testament-soaked, but does that fact alone make the claim 'Jesus has been raised from the dead' an easy sell? Not exactly. In this chapter, I want us to think about (1) what exactly it was that Peter's audience believed about the resurrection *before* he started to speak; and (2) how Peter's speech might have confirmed, extended and even radically altered their expectations regarding the resurrection. Because the truth is, once a man stands up in Jerusalem and says that his guy has risen from the dead and therefore he's the Messiah, there is still a *lot* of heavy lifting to do. Jewish people in the first century were expecting a lot of things—but no-one we know of was expecting *that*.

The Old Testament and the afterlife

You see, contrary to popular belief, the Old Testament doesn't have a whole lot to say about life after death. If religion is supposed to be all about death and the afterlife, the Jewish people missed the memo. At a broad level, the Old Testament just isn't about that topic—at least not directly. And, what's more, when the Old Testament does talk about the afterlife, what it says is often oblique and almost always negative. I was once engaged in a public dialogue with a Jewish Rabbi, who was gently chastising us Gentiles for our sentimental attitudes to death. "Judaism is about life!" he exclaimed. "We *hate* death."

Let me show you what I mean. Consider, for example, the many psalms in which the psalmist pleads with God to spare his life, because being dead is a Really Bad Idea:

> For in death there is no remembrance of you;
>> in Sheol who will give you praise? (Ps 6:5)

> "What profit is there in my death,
>> if I go down to the pit?
> Will the dust praise you?
>> Will it tell of your faithfulness?" (Ps 30:9)

> The dead do not praise the LORD,
>> Nor do any who go down into silence. (Ps 115:17)

Notice the way death in these psalms is an entirely negative outcome. It is a state in which nobody wins: the psalmist becomes dust, and God is not praised. The attitude of the psalmist is never, "Oh, hello Death. My whole religion prepared me to meet you with peace and confidence". It's much more, "Death! No way. I'm an Israelite—get me out of here!"

Some Old Testament writers appear to have no hope of any conscious existence beyond the grave at all. Consider, for example, Ecclesiastes:

> This is an evil in all that is done under the sun, that the same event happens to all. Also, the hearts of the children of man are full of evil, and madness is in their hearts while they live, and after that they go to the dead. But he who is joined with all the living has hope, for a living dog is better than a dead lion. For the living know that they will die, but the dead know nothing, and they have no more reward, for the memory of them is forgotten. Their love and their hate and their envy have already perished, and forever they have no more share in all that is done under the sun...
>
> Whatever your hand finds to do, do it with your might, for there is no work or thought or knowledge or wisdom in Sheol, to which you are going. (Eccl 9:3-6, 10)

Other Old Testament writers see some sort of consciousness in the place of the dead, in Sheol, but it's a long way from eternal bliss. For example, consider the words of Isaiah, the prophet to the Babylonian rulers, concerning what they can expect at their death:

> "Sheol beneath is stirred up
>   to meet you when you come;
> it rouses the shades to greet you,
>   all who were leaders of the earth;

> it raises from their thrones
>> all who were kings of the nations.
> All of them will answer
>> and say to you:
> 'You too have become as weak as we!
>> You have become like us!'" (Isa 14:9-10)

Notice how vague and ethereal it all is. These once great kings, now stirred from their sad slumber in Sheol, weak and ghoulish.

There are some intriguing cases in the Old Testament of communication with the dead (something regularly forbidden)—most famously the case of Samuel, whose spirit is disturbed by the witch at Endor (1 Sam 28:3-25). But there is little in the Old Testament on what that state is actually like, and almost nothing to suggest that Sheol, the place of the dead, is a place of blessing or an object of hope. Sheol is not a hope to long for, but a place to be rescued from. And the Old Testament says virtually nothing about 'heaven', at least as we popularly conceive it as the place we go to be with God when we die.[16] Remember the Rabbi? "Judaism is about life! We *hate* death." Sounds like the words of someone who knows their Old Testament.

"But what about resurrection in the Old Testament?" I hear you say. And you are right. There are a number of places in the Old Testament that do talk explicitly about the resurrection. Chief among them is Daniel 12:2-3:

---

16   More on this in chapter 5.

"And many of those who sleep in the dust of the earth shall awake, some to everlasting life, and some to shame and everlasting contempt. And those who are wise shall shine like the brightness of the sky above; and those who turn many to righteousness, like the stars forever and ever."

Undeniably, here you have a statement of resurrection belief. It comes as God's answer to the cry of the psalmist. To the palmist's plea, "Who praises you from the grave?" God's answer is, "No-one—therefore, I will raise you up". 'Resurrection', you see, is not a word that means the nice side of the afterlife. It does not re-cast death; it casts off death. Resurrection is a rescue *from* the grave, not a refurbishment *of* the grave.

By the time of Jesus, the hope of the resurrection is the orthodox Jewish understanding. But it is not the only option on the table—the Sadducees, for example, did not accept it.[17] And the wider point is that life after death is a minor plot line in the Old Testament, not the major obsession we might assume it is. It was something that divided one school of Jewish thought from another, rather than a core thing on which they all agreed.

---

17 The Sadducees, according to Acts 23:7-9, didn't believe in spirits, angels or resurrections.

The rising Messiah?

The second great obstacle for Peter's message on that day in Jerusalem was that the idea of the Messiah rising from the dead simple wasn't, as far as we know, on the table for anyone. There were many messianic claimants around the time of Jesus. If 'rising from the dead' was a thing the Messiah was supposed to do, then you can be sure that every man and his dog would be, *Weekend at Bernie's*-style[18], working on elaborate schemes for proving that their guy rose. But, apart from the Christians, no-one did that. Why? Because in the first century, if you said, "Hey! Our guy rose from the dead", you would eventually get the reply, "And...?" No-one would fill in that blank with "Therefore he's the Messiah". It was a case you had to argue *for,* not something you could argue *from.*[19]

So then, why does Peter's speech get such a good reception from the crowd on that day? I have tried to argue that:

a. Life after death isn't the major concern of the Old Testament.

b. A general resurrection of the righteous and the unrighteous is the hope on which the Old Testament eventually lands (Dan 12:2-3).

---

18 *Weekend at Bernie's* being a forgettable 1980s comedy in which the protagonists carry around the body of the recently deceased Bernie, pretending he is still alive so that (I seem to recall) they could keep using his holiday house. The '80s were deeply troubled times.

19 For detailed discussion on this point of the rising Messiah, see NT Wright, *The Resurrection of the Son of God,* SPCK, London, 2003, pp. 204-6.

c. No-one we know of around the time of Jesus expected a resurrection of a single individual in history, and no-one expected that of the Messiah.

What, then, was Peter's speech drawing on? If they were divided on the "What happens when you die?" question, why was he able to make such sense of a resurrection? And if rising from the dead was on no-one's job description at the time, how was he able to persuade so many that (a) resurrection is what happened to Jesus; and (b) that this meant he was the Messiah?

To attempt an answer, let me have a shot at getting into the head of one of Peter's listeners on that day. What did they believe? What story did they tell themselves? How did the story Peter was telling plug so readily into the story they believed they were living? Well, based on the story they all knew so well from Genesis to the end of 2 Kings and beyond, *and understood through the prism of their present experience*, their view of the world and themselves would have looked a little something like this:

Our God is the Lord of Heaven and Earth. He made this world, he made us, and he chose Israel. Our father Abraham was chosen by God so that we, his descendants, could bring the blessings of God to the world to the Gentiles. God's promises to Abraham were that, through him and through his children, all nations would be blessed. And we would be great.

But our story has been a rocky one. Abraham had Isaac, and Isaac had Jacob, and Jacob had twelve sons. And those sons tried to kill their brother Joseph and they threw him down into a pit. His brothers and his father thought he was dead.

But God raised him up. God lifted him out of the pit and brought him into the land of Egypt. He was taken to Egypt as a slave, but he was bought by an Egyptian, and God gave him success and lifted him up, and the Lord blessed the household of the Egyptian through Joseph. But there was a plot against Joseph and he was thrown into prison and he languished there.

But God raised him up again. He brought Joseph from prison to be the Prime Minister of Egypt. And through his wisdom and power and faithfulness, he saw that a famine was coming. Under his direction Egypt saved so much grain that it was able to feed the world. All nations were blessed through Joseph.

But after Pharaoh there arose another who did not know Joseph, and our people were enslaved in Egypt for 400 years. But God sent us Moses, and through Moses he raised us up out of Egypt and carried us on eagle's wings to Mount Sinai. And there God made a covenant with us. He gave us the law, and he made us priests of the whole earth, so that the whole earth could know our God through us.

And God took us into the land, and he gave us a great king—King David. And David first suffered— he was chased by his enemies—and then was crowned with glory. God was with him and made him the Anointed One of Israel, the Messiah. And God promised that a Son of David would rule Israel forever and bring blessing to the nations.

Solomon was that great son. He sat on David's throne. And we were wealthy, and we were wise, and we were at peace, and we had a temple. And just as God had promised, the nations began to stream into Jerusalem to hear the wisdom of David's son, and to see his splendour. And they could see that God was with us. We were a city on a hill. We were the light of the world.

But then it all came unstuck. Solomon and his sons walked away from the Lord. They became corrupt, and we did not follow the covenant and commands of the Lord. And we were warned by the prophets, again and again, that if we did not return to the covenant, we would be cast out of the land just as Adam and Eve were cast out of Eden. And we did not listen.

Israel was divided into two separate 'kingdoms'— ten tribes forming a northern kingdom known as Israel, and two tribes forming a southern kingdom called Judah. The Northern Kingdom was destroyed by the Assyrians, and 200 years later the South, Judah, was taken into exile by the Babylonians. Our king, Zedekiah, the son of David, had his eyes plucked out and was led blind and chained into Babylon. And for 70 years we were humiliated. The nation that had been rescued from slavery in Egypt had now been sent back into slavery in Babylon.

Sometimes we were angry, and we sang songs of revenge and vindication. But mostly we were sad. We wept. The dream was over. And (as the prophets kept telling us) it was all our own fault.

But then, in the community in exile a rumour started to spread. Word started to filter through from the prophets that there was life on the other side of our nation's death. That even though we had broken

*the covenant, God was going to do something for us.
That God was going to raise us up and do something
new with us and through us.*

*One of our prophets, Ezekiel, said it was as if
Israel was a valley of dry bones. It was as if we had
died as a nation. But he saw us, this valley of dry
bones, being breathed on by the breath of God, just as
Adam had received the breath of God in the garden.
And the prophet saw all the bones coming together
again, and he saw tissue and muscles begin to form
on the bones, and he saw skin and bodies coming
together. And there they were—a mighty and vast
army. And God breathed into them the breath of life.
And they stood, and they lived.*

*And it was us! We were that army. Us! Refugees!
We were going to stand again.*

*And we did. God sent Cyrus, and through him
we were returned to our land.[20] And we built a new
temple. And we began home rule again. And we were
a nation again!*

Sort of. In a way. If you squinted.

*Because, to be honest, since returning to the land
it has not been great. We've had some high points
but, actually, for most of the time we've been under
foreign rule. We have been trampled on and taken
over and beaten up. To be honest, we thought it was
going to be more than this. God seemed to be saying
that through us he was going to bring redemption to*

---

20 Cyrus was the Persian ruler who returned the Jews to Israel from
Babylon.

the world—even a new heaven and a new earth; the
end of all conflict; the Spirit poured out on all flesh;
and the forgiveness of sins. We thought God had
promised that David's son would come and make us
a nation again. And that hasn't happened.

Yet.

Peter in Jerusalem

That, or something very like it, was the sort of story that the people listening to Peter in Jerusalem had in their heads. At least, that's the story faithful Israel had in its head. We're introduced to a number of faithful Israelites at the beginning of Luke's Gospel (which, being written by the same guy, is really volume 1 of Luke-Acts). We meet people like Anna, Simeon, Joseph and Mary—people who longed for the consolation of Israel, the redemption of Jerusalem.

Because when someone has made you a promise, and the promise hasn't come through yet, you have a couple of options. You can abandon the promise, deciding that the one who made it just hasn't come through. You can fudge the promise and decide that whatever has happened now is a rough approximation of the promise, and it will have to do.

Or you can wait.

At school, I was never very good at sport. It's a genetic thing. It didn't particularly trouble me. But I distinctly remember one day when, at a school sports carnival, I ran the 1500-metre race and came a predictable second-last. That didn't worry me. What did worry me was that as the stickers for first, second and third place were proudly attached to the t-shirts of the winners, the rest of us were given stickers that said, "I did my best".

Even then, at age seven, I felt the insult. I had come second-last. And the school declared, in effect, "This is as much as we ever expect from this boy. A poor result by any objective measure, but the best he can do".

At the time of the New Testament, we find a group of people who refuse to say to God, "You did your best". We meet people like Mary and Joseph and the gang, who remember what God promised the exiles and who kept saying to themselves and to each other, "This can't be what God meant. This can't be God's best." That is, they are the people Jesus describes in the Sermon on the Mount: "Blessed are the poor in spirit..." (Matt 5:3).

Now, consider Peter's speech from that angle. What is Peter saying? First, Peter says (Acts 2:16f): This is it! This is *that* time—the promise God made to us all those years ago is coming in *now*. God is keeping his promise that he would come and restore Israel, and pour out his Spirit on all people, and forgive our sins. This is that.

Secondly, Peter continues (verse 22 onwards), we all made a big mistake with Jesus. Jesus was accredited to us by God through signs and miracles. We handed him over to death, *but God raised him up*. Remember? God had promised to put one of David's descendants on his throne. Which one? Not Solomon, but the one David was prophesying about when he said in the psalms, "you will not abandon my soul to Sheol, or let your holy one see corruption" (Ps 16:10). That was David speaking about the Messiah! God raised up Jesus—and that means that he's the one. The time of our exile has ended. The Kingdom has come. The Messiah has come. Let all Israel be assured of this: "God has made this Jesus, whom you crucified, both Lord and Messiah!" (Acts 2:36, HCSB).

The resurrection doesn't *make* Jesus into the second person of the trinity, God the Son. God the Son has been God the Son from all eternity. But it does *enthrone* Jesus of Nazareth, God the Son incarnate, as both Lord and Messiah. It establishes him as the true king of Israel (Messiah) and therefore as the rightful ruler of all creation (Lord). At the incarnation, God the Son became the man Jesus of Nazareth. At the resurrection, the incarnate Son became both Lord and Christ. (If you can bear in mind that the phrase 'God the Son' refers to the eternal second member of the trinity, whereas the phrase 'the Son of God' in the Bible refers almost always to the King or Messiah of Israel [see 2 Samuel 7:14, Psalm 2:7], you could put it like this: At the resurrection, God the Son became the Son of God.)

Understanding this hope

Here's where I'm trying to take this.

Firstly, there are Old Testament passages that affirm the hope of the resurrection. Not heaps. Not all over the place. But they are there, and like a dry Australian forest

RAISED FOREVER

in late summer, you only have to put a match to them for them to burst into flame.

Secondly, and more importantly, there is a whole shape of Old Testament story into which the resurrection of Jesus fits. The claims of the New Testament don't rely on a kind of 'Where's Wally?' approach to the Old Testament. Raising up Israel, and vindicating and restoring Israel, is what God does. The big surprise is not that God can raise people from the dead, but that he's done it *now*, in history, with this guy—with Jesus. It's surprising but, once you get over the initial shock, what it must mean can be plugged pretty readily into what you already know about God and the way he operates.

Thirdly, notice how simple Peter's resurrection theology is. There are two verdicts on Jesus:

1. We thought he was worthy of crucifixion.
2. God thinks he is worthy of resurrection.

From that day in Jerusalem through to this day, those two verdicts haunt everyone who has ever considered the claims of Jesus. We thought he deserved to be crucified. God contradicted that verdict. Now, there are two opposite verdicts on Jesus out there: ours and God's. Which are you going to choose?

Over the last two chapters we have looked at two vastly different sermons, shaped by their distinctive contexts. As far as contexts go, Athens and Jerusalem are about as different as you could imagine. But precisely because they are so different, they provide something of a control experiment for us to ask an important question: what is the *essential* gospel message? Allowing for all the cultural, personal and historical differences, what do you have to say to have (in any meaningful sense) proclaimed the gospel?

And the answer from Acts 2 and Acts 17 is simply this: by virtue of his resurrection from the dead, Jesus is Lord (2:36, 17:30-31).

That is where both speeches land. That is the gospel message to both religious Jews and sceptical pagans. The gospel message is not fundamentally about us and our needs, but about Jesus and his status. The gospel is not a suggestion ("Have you ever considered Jesus?"), nor is it advice ("You know, things really would be better if you included Jesus"), nor is it a plea ("Hey, everyone, vote for Jesus"). It is, at heart, news. It is *gospel*. And the news is that Jesus is Lord.

It is impossible to imagine that someone who heard either Peter or Paul's sermon could then testify at a youth group camp years later: "Back then, I think I knew Jesus as my Saviour but not as my Lord". The Saviour-but-not-Lord proposition was not even on the table. The message to which they were invited to respond *was* the message of the lordship of Jesus *and nothing else*. Jesus can save and judge and forgive and restore *because* he is Lord. None of those are separate things that you can add on to Jesus in the way you can upgrade software. Judging, saving, forgiving and restoring—they are all part of the job description captured in the phrase 'Jesus is Lord'.

This is a message from which Paul never wavered. Notice his summary of the gospel message, with which he begins his letter to the Romans:

> ...the gospel of God, which he promised beforehand through his prophets in the holy Scriptures, concerning his Son, who was descended from David according to the flesh and was declared to be the Son of God in power according to the Spirit of holiness by his resurrection from the dead, Jesus Christ our Lord. (Rom 1:1-4)

You see: no resurrection, no gospel. Later in the same letter, Paul says "the word of faith that we proclaim" is: "If you confess with your mouth that Jesus is Lord and believe in your heart that God raised him from the dead, you will be saved" (Rom 10:7, 9). And toward the end of his life, Paul is still able to summarize his message as "...Jesus Christ, risen from the dead, the offspring of David, as preached in my gospel" (2 Tim 2:8).

Compared to the New Testament, our relative lack of emphasis on the resurrection of Jesus is utterly obscure. The resurrection declares the lordship of Jesus, which is the heart of the gospel message. And the corollary of that declaration is the invitation to 'repent' (Acts 2:37-38, 17:30).

To repent is most literally to change your mind. In the context of the gospel message, it is to admit that if the Creator God has declared Jesus to be Lord, and he is not also at the same time *your* Lord, then that needs to change. The times of forgiveness and refreshment and the outpouring of the Spirit have come—so repent (2:38-39). The times in which God would overlook idolatry have ended—so repent (17:30). Different context; same message.

In Jesus' resurrection God has played his hand, so change your mind. God's verdict on Jesus is very simple: he's Lord. If that is not also your verdict on Jesus (in your heart and in your life), then you have a major difference of opinion with your Creator. And as a general rule of thumb, if you find yourself in disagreement with your Creator, you don't wait to see who blinks first. You change your mind in accordance with reality. To become a Christian is to follow this simple logic: if Jesus has been declared *the* Lord, he ought also to be *my* Lord.

Chapter 3

THE EMPTY TOMB

Will convert for evidence

At a recent Atheist-Christian dialogue, I saw a man with a T-shirt saying, 'Will Convert for Evidence.' As a statement, it captures a common objection to religion in general and Christianity in particular—namely, that it demands 'faith', not evidence. Take, for example, Richard Dawkins' words:

> Faith is the great cop-out, the great excuse to evade the need to think and evaluate evidence. Faith is belief in spite of, even perhaps because of, the lack of evidence.[21]

---

21 R Dawkins, 'Lecture from "The Nullifidian" (Dec 94)', The Richard Dawkins Foundation for Reason and Science, Falcon, CO, 11 May 2006 (viewed 10 September 2013): http://old.richarddawkins.net/articles/89

This, according to Dawkins and many others, is why religion is positively dangerous. It is a toxic mix of high loyalty and low reason, a force at work in the world unhinged from critical thinking and careful evaluation of truth claims. Belief apart from evidence is the great bug in the software of all religious faith. Because of this bug (to mix a metaphor), religion poisons everything.

On the other hand, some Christians would argue that belief without evidence is not a bug, but a feature. Accepting the premise, they see faith as going where reason may not. They believe that faith is, at its heart, a leap into the epistemic darkness that God positively encourages, indeed commands. "If there were proof, we wouldn't need faith."

And my question is, when it comes to the Christian gospel, is that true? Are either of those claims true? Does a belief in the Christian gospel require a person to believe in spite of evidence? If someone comes to church and asks a Christian, "Is your faith based on anything?", must we simply reply, "Oh, you mean evidence? We don't go in for that sort of thing around here"?

Athens, Jerusalem and the tomb

What we have looked at so far in this book is preaching. In particular, we have looked at two sermons declaring, in their own ways, that (a) Jesus Christ was raised from the dead; and that (b) this means that he is both Lord and Christ. In both cases, resurrection is something that was argued *from*, not *for*. The shape of the case has been: given the resurrection of Jesus, you ought to repent.

The resurrection of Jesus is clearly something the New Testament writers think *proves* something, but can the resurrection itself be proved? This is what I'd like to think about in this chapter.

The claim we are considering here is simple. Well, it's simple to grasp. It is that at some stage in the very early morning, on the first day of the week (we call that day Sunday), sometime in the early Spring (in a month we call April), **Jesus, who was dead, left behind an empty tomb because his body had been raised and he was now alive and appearing to his disciples**. That's the claim. That's what the early Christians believed happened to Jesus. What caused that belief? To explore this question, we need to consider three things:

1. the background against which this belief arose
2. the nature of the evidence available to us
3. the force of that evidence.

1. Background

Considering first the background question, we can say something pretty certain here: resurrection was on nobody's job description we know of in the first century. It is a point sometimes missed, but it is crucial. We've touched on this earlier, but let's gather together the evidence to make things crystal clear.

The pagan world

Consider the cultured pagans Paul was speaking to in Athens that day. The Greco-Roman culture had many and various traditions about what happened or could happen to people when they died. In his seminal study on the topic, historian NT Wright has worked painstakingly through the ancient literature on the topic. The pagan world had rich and varied traditions on the fate of the dead: it had traditions of spirits going to live in a murky underworld, traditions of people coming back as ghosts, and traditions where people simply died and were no more. There is even a strange little story of Apollonius of Tyana who may or may not have successfully brought back to life a dead (or deadish) girl before her wedding—though whether she was really dead or not is (says the author of the story) "a mysterious problem which neither I myself nor those who were present could decide".[22] There were many and various options available to you on the question of what happens when you die, but overwhelmingly resurrection wasn't one of them. In *Eumenides*, Apollo, at the founding of the Areopagus (the very place Paul was speaking), says:

> Once a man has died, and the dust has soaked up his blood, there is no resurrection.[23]

In fact, not only did no-one we know of believe in

---

22 *Life of Apollonius of Tyana*, 4:45, cited in NT Wright, *The Resurrection of the Son of God*, SPCK, London, 2003, p. 74.

23 Cited in Wright, *Resurrection of the Son of God*, p. 32.

resurrection, almost everything else in Greek thought made the idea not only unthinkable, but also unattractive. With no traditions of a creator God, their whole relationship to the material world and to human bodies in particular was complex and often hostile. Bodies were things to be escaped from, not something you wanted hanging around like a bad smell in the next life.

Now, to be sure, there were in that world traditions of dying and rising gods—Adonis, Attis, Dionysus, and so on. But these are precisely gods, not humans. These traditions did not involve human bodies. And they did not happen in our time, but in the 'dreamtime'—the mythic era. Moreover, they were associated with cyclical patterns of winter and spring and harvest. They are stories about how things are, not (as in Christian theology) a radical intrusion into our world of how things could be. If you asked an ancient pagan, "So, when did Adonis rise, and who witnessed it, and who was in government at the time?" they would give you a puzzled look back and say, "Um, you don't really get myth, do you?" When Paul was in Athens proclaiming the resurrection of the man Jesus, no-one said, "This sounds familiar. We have stories like this." They thought it was absurd.[24]

In summary, in pagan thought, humans might have been expected to do lots of things, or no things, when they died: the one thing they were *never* expected to do is rise from the dead. The belief 'Jesus rose from the dead'

---

24 Wright, *Resurrection of the Son of God*, p. 81.

can't have been a belief nurtured in pagan soil. Asking the historian's question, "Where did this Christian belief about Jesus come from?", we can be confident that wherever it came from, it wasn't from the expectations of paganism.

Jewish culture

What about Jewish culture? As we saw in the last chapter, Jewish thought did have within it a tradition of resurrection. Belief in a good God who made this material universe and might want to redeem it made it thinkable, the shape of their story made it plausible (again, as we saw in the previous chapter), and some specific scriptural promises in Daniel and elsewhere made it believable.

But here's the thing. For those who believed in a coming resurrection of the dead, there was a very strict timetable: life lived in a veil of tears now, resurrection in the age to come then. Many believed that the resurrection of the dead would usher in the new age; but *no-one* expected a single person to be raised in history. Martha speaks for the majority when, in reply to Jesus' claim that her brother will rise again, she says, "I know that he will rise again in the resurrection on the last day" (John 11:24).

It's a crucial point because in claiming that Jesus was raised from the dead, the early Christians weren't making their job easier. There wasn't a figure in people's minds who everyone knew would rise from the dead, such that Christians could say "Our guy is *that* guy". The claim that someone rose to resurrection life in this age was novel, and raised as many questions as it answered.

To summarize: resurrection hope in general is clearly Jewish rather than pagan. However, the specific claim that (a) one man was raised in history, and (b) he was therefore the Messiah, was unprecedented. To quote Wright again:

> The world of Judaism had generated, from its rich scriptural origins, a rich variety of beliefs about what happened, and would happen, to the dead. But it was quite unprepared for the new mutation that sprang up, like a totally unexpected plant, within that already well-stocked garden.[25]

It seems, in short, that the Christian belief in the resurrection of Jesus was not *caused* by the already extablished expectations of paganism or Judaism. It must have been caused by something else. What caused it? Herodotus, the father of history, tells us that he wrote his history of the wars between the Greeks and the rest not just as a record of "the facts" but in order to "give the *cause* of their fighting one another". In his seminal work on the nature of history, EH Carr affirms that the "study of history is the study of causes".[26] Historians do not just ask "What?"; they must also ask "Why?", by which they normally mean, "What caused this?" For us, we know the early Christians believed Jesus was raised from the dead. What caused this belief? The Christian claim, of course, is that belief *in* the resurrection of Jesus was caused by the event *of* the resurrection of Jesus.

---

25 Wright, *Resurrection of the Son of God*, p. 206.
26 EH Carr, *What is History?*, Penguin Books, London, 1964, p. 87.

2. The evidence

But do we have any evidence for such an event? And what sort of evidence do we have?

The answer is that we have *historical* evidence. That is, we don't have *scientific* evidence. There aren't labs in Oxford at the moment testing the hypothesis that if a dead male Jewish body is placed in a sufficiently cool tomb for between 48 and 72 hours, it may be expected to rise. The nature of the claim is not scientific, and therefore the nature of the evidence is not scientific.[27] But that doesn't mean that the evidence is *religious* or *faith-based*. This is not a claim about something that happened in the dreamtime, or in mythology, or in our hearts. It is an historical claim, for which we have historical evidence, with all the sorts of certainties, probabilities and ambiguities that any historical evidence affords. And when we are talking historical evidence, we are talking texts.

What sorts of texts? Who wrote them?

The most common question here is, "Did any non-Christian writers have anything to say about Jesus?" The

---

27 Unless of course you are one of those people who has decided to use the word 'scientific' to incorporate a wide and disparate body of phenomena including critical thinking, reason, experimentation, secularism and any other number of things that are, well, true. It's your language too. Knock yourself out. Just don't come back whinging to me when you're looking for a word to describe the process of hypothesis, experimentation and verification to which the word 'scientific' used to refer. In a world where the word 'literally' can mean 'added emphasis' (as in "I literally was dying with laughter"), all bets are off.

answer is yes. The truth is, you could get a fair bit of information about Jesus even if every source written by a believer suddenly vanished from the earth. You could work out, for example, that Jesus was a noted teacher, that he had a reputation for miracles or sorcery, and that he died by crucifixion under Pontius Pilate.[28]

However, the truth is that *most* of what we know about Jesus and almost everything we know about his resurrection comes from the writings of his followers. Is that a problem? Emphatically, no. To dismiss any historical source on the basis that it is biased would be a decision to cease the discipline of history altogether. What source is not biased? Sources will have relative value, and it is the job of the historian to weigh their value according to the canons of their discipline, but no historical source is entirely free from the commitments of its author.

And neither should it be. Who of us, on picking up a biography of, say, Mahatma Gandhi, would throw it away in disgust having discovered that the author actually liked Gandhi, or was a pacifist, or shared the opinion that British Colonial rule in India was unjust. On the contrary, it would be surprising if a biography of Gandhi was written by someone with little to no enthusiasm for Ghandi. Of course, we would weigh what they say in light of their commitments, we would test their claims

---

28 For a crisp summary, see J Dickson, *A Spectator's Guide to Jesus: An Introduction to the Man from Nazareth*, Blue Bottle Books, Sydney, 2005, pp. 9-22.

against primary sources, and we would evaluate their arguments against other accounts. But that is a long way from the frankly lazy statement, "That evidence comes from Christians, therefore I discount it".

Just one source?

The other myth we can gently set aside here is the idea that 'The Bible' is one source, and that it shares all the fragility and precariousness of other claims coming from a single source or person. The truth is, that thing we call 'the Bible' and the section we call the 'New Testament' is in fact a collection of writings, written by many authors— authors who, in some cases, are themselves drawing on many sources before them.

The main writings containing relevant data concerning Jesus come to us from Matthew, Mark, Luke, John and Paul. Luke tells us at the beginning of his Gospel that "many have undertaken to compile a narrative of the things that have been accomplished among us" (Luke 1:1). That is, Luke is not the first cab off the rank; he is writing his own account through the use of others. As scholars have sifted painstakingly through the Gospels, they have discerned at least some of those sources.

Matthew, for example, draws on a source known as 'M', with material found in no other Gospel. Mark (likely the earliest of the Gospels) seems to have been available to both Matthew and Luke as one of their sources. Luke draws on a source or sources called 'L'. And both Matthew and Luke draw on a source we call 'Q', which

Mark did not seem to have access to.[29] And John—well, John is paddling his own canoe. 'Q', so far as we can work out, ends before Jesus arrives in Jerusalem. On a conservative count, that leaves us with Mark, 'L', 'M', and John as independent witnesses to the death, burial, empty tomb and appearances of Jesus.[30]

For Christians, these sources and the ways the Gospels sometimes rub up against each other can seem awkward. It is sometimes very hard to reconcile the various supposed discrepancies between the accounts. But what might be awkward for Christians is thrilling for historians, because such things are proof positive that there was no central command, no conspiratorial council of later Christians who huddled together and ironed out all the difficulties. No-one has cooked the books. Religious neat-nicks might wish someone had, but people interested in history are glad they didn't. It assures us that we have multiple independent sources. In historiography, multiplicity and independence are precious jewels.

---

29 Those letters 'M' and 'L' are just shorthand for 'stuff that Matthew or Luke have access to that the other guys don't seem to have access to.' Not the most creative names, I know. And, just in case you thought New Testament scholars suddenly got all arty and creative with the label 'Q', it's just the first letter of the German word for source. The point here is that if you are trying to think of a name for your band or your first child, I wouldn't bother asking New Testament scholars for advice.

30 For discussion see P Barnett, *Gospel Truth: Answering the New Atheist Attacks on the Gospels*, IVP, Nottingham, 2012, pp. 131-6. The 'M' source, as Barnett notes, does not refer to the empty tomb, though we may assume that an empty tomb is taken for granted by the resurrection appearances.

I also mentioned Paul. Why Paul? Few of us would naturally think of Paul as a major source for the historical details of the life of Jesus. Many Christians assume that the Gospels are where you go for 'the facts', and Paul is where you find the theology. But on the contrary, just as the Gospels are chock-full of theology, so Paul is chock-full of facts. And his witness is especially precious to historians for at least three reasons: (1) it is early; (2) it is incidental; and (3) it constitutes (in a weird way) an eyewitness account.

First, it's early. The Gospels are difficult to date, and it is probable that material within them is from sources very close to Jesus indeed. But in the case of Paul, we are certain that his writings were written between 49 and 64 AD, giving us witnesses to within 20 years of the events they describe.

Second, it's incidental. By this we mean that Paul never sat down to write a life of Jesus. He did not aim to clarify historical points about Jesus' life, nor did he write with one eye on future historians sifting through his material. Rather, Paul wrote to churches to address various confusions on points of doctrine, practice or morality. Why is this good? Well, imagine that 100 years from now historians were desperate to know what you *really* thought of the F Scott Fitzgerald novel *The Great Gatsby*. If they had an essay you wrote for high school English in which you praised the work, that would be something. But, of course, you might have just been trying to say what the teacher wanted to hear to get good marks. But imagine if they also found an email from you to another friend about the coming school holidays in which you mentioned, incidentally, that you'd lend them *The Great Gatsby* over the summer because you really enjoyed it. For historians, that email would be much more valuable evidence than the essay, precisely because of its incidental nature. Paul's testimony to the historical details of Jesus' life is more like the email than the essay.

Third, it's from an eyewitness. Paul was not an eyewitness to the empty tomb, but he did consider himself an eyewitness to the risen Christ. His claim to this title is unusual: he was not one of those who saw Jesus in the days in Israel between his resurrection and ascension. His witness was on the road to Damascus, after Jesus' ascension. He is aware that this makes him the exception, the "one untimely born" (1 Cor 15:8), but neither did he consider his encounter with Jesus a mere vision or religious experience. It qualified him as an apostle (1 Cor 9:1), and the other apostles accepted this to be the case (Gal 1:18-24).

1 Corinthians 15:1-11

With all that in place, let's look at an actual text. There are many places we could go, but in terms of resurrection texts, 1 Corinthians 15:1-11 is Grand Central Station. All traffic must come through here. It was written in 54 AD and it was written, as it were, as an aside (the point of the chapter is really in verses 12 and following, verses 1-11 being a rehearsal of some uncontested teaching). It says:

> Now I would remind you, brothers, of the gospel I
> preached to you, which you received, in which you

stand, [2] and by which you are being saved, if you hold fast to the word I preached to you—unless you believed in vain.

[3] For I delivered to you as of first importance what I also received: that Christ died for our sins in accordance with the Scriptures, [4] that he was buried, that he was raised on the third day in accordance with the Scriptures, [5] and that he appeared to Cephas, then to the twelve. [6] Then he appeared to more than five hundred brothers at one time, most of whom are still alive, though some have fallen asleep. [7] Then he appeared to James, then to all the apostles. [8] Last of all, as to one untimely born, he appeared also to me. [9] For I am the least of the apostles, unworthy to be called an apostle, because I persecuted the church of God. [10] But by the grace of God I am what I am, and his grace toward me was not in vain. On the contrary, I worked harder than any of them, though it was not I, but the grace of God that is with me. [11] Whether then it was I or they, so we preach and so you believed.

Notice what sort of account this is. It's not poetry. It's not something that is really designed to stir the heart. It's not rich with metaphor and allusion. You couldn't imagine singing it. It's fussy. It's about who was where when: First this guy, then that guy, then the other. You have names: Cephas, James, Paul. You have numbers: the 12 and the 500. And you have that strange detail: That most of the 500 are still alive.

Why include that? At least part of it, surely, is to remind the Corinthians that they could still talk to those witnesses about what they saw.

It is close to the time. Did you notice that Paul says this is something he "received" (v. 3)? First Corinthians was written within about 20 years of the events in question, but Paul is drawing on traditions that go back much earlier. If, as seems likely, Paul received this tradition from the Christians in Jerusalem—maybe at his baptism in 34 AD or his first visit to Jerusalem in 36 AD—then we are talking about information *very* close to the events it reports.[31] That is, it is too close to the time of the original events for anyone to plausibly suggest that 'resurrection' is something later Christians attached to the Jesus story as they were writing the Gospels.

The Gospels

When we move forward from Paul to the Gospels, significant details are added. For example, only men are mentioned in Paul's writings. But in the Gospels, we read about women arriving first at the empty tomb. Paul likely leaves out the women because in first century culture, women's testimony was not readily accepted. The Gospel writers likely include them because when it comes to telling the story, like it or not, everyone knew that is what happened.

You have details of a garden tomb, and information about the time of the day. You have names: Mary, the other Mary, Salome, Joanna, John (universally believed

---

31 For discussion of these points, see Barnett, *Gospel Truth*, pp. 129-31.

to be "the other disciple" mentioned in John 20), Peter and Cleopas.

You have gratuitous information: stones, folded linen, who arrived at the tomb first, and who went in first. And you have in these accounts an impressive circumspection about things that would have been tempting to expand on, but which, without witnesses, no-one felt at liberty to embellish. For example, no-one actually describes the resurrection moment itself. Others in later centuries tried to fill in this gap by writing up imagined accounts of the actual moment of resurrection,[32] but in the early biblical accounts, there is no such thing. Presumably no-one saw it, and therefore no-one wrote it.

And you have awkward disagreements. Who arrived when, how many women were there, and who saw appearances of Jesus where and when? Many have been intrigued by these disagreements and have offered fascinating and plausible reconciliations.[33] But there they are: a permanent testimony to the fact that no fussy group ever got their hands on these documents to tidy them all up.

---

32 If you're curious, have a look at the so-called *Gospel of Peter*. Verses 35-42 are where the author really lets himself go (I don't suppose I have to say this wasn't actually written by Peter?). It's available online (viewed 1 June 2014): http://earlychristianwritings.com/text/gospelpeter-brown.html

33 See for example J Wenham's *Easter Enigma: Are the Resurrection Accounts in Conflict?*, Wipf & Stock, London, 2005, or the appendices of M Jensen's *Alive with Christ*, Matthias Media, Sydney, 2013.

Empty tomb and appearances

Looking at these sources, I think we can be confident of two data-points:

1. The tomb was found empty.
2. Jesus' followers started to report appearances.

What do you do with that? Neither one nor the other, taken in isolation, would have given rise to the early Christian claims of the resurrection of Jesus. Bereaved people having visions of a recently lost loved one is a commonplace of human experience. Just last week I talked with someone who had precisely this experience. They are common now and they were common then. And the tacit assumption of anyone who has this experience is that the body of the loved one remains where it was buried.

Conversely, the discovery of an empty tomb could not, on its own, secure the widespread belief that the body had been raised. So many other explanations commend themselves first: grave robbers, mistaken tombs, tricksters. And besides, no-one's sacred texts or religious traditions knew what to do with a single empty tomb. The multitudes sleeping in the dust of the earth being raised at the end of time? Sure. A single individual leaving behind an empty tomb in history? Not on anyone's list of religious expectations.

But of course, these data-points are not isolated. The reality of the empty tomb *and* the claims about Jesus appearing co-exist. That becomes much harder to explain away.

Could you account for these two things in some other way? Sure. Let's think about that.

For example, if Jesus wasn't really dead, you could account for both facts (empty tomb and appearances). Perhaps he merely 'swooned' on the cross. If he had gone unconscious and then in the coolness of the tomb revived, then you could account for both facts. Not a problem.

A mistaken tomb would also do the trick. You come to a tomb that you could have sworn was the place Jesus was buried, and then, with a mixture of imagination and grief, the appearances start and you begin to put two and two together. That would also account for the facts of the case.

Or perhaps the body was stolen—right tomb, but too late. This is, in fact, the oldest explanation we have. It was the women's first thought when they saw the empty tomb (John 20:2). Was it the Romans? The Jewish authorities? Or maybe his followers themselves stole it and then made up the story of Jesus being raised from the dead. A tomb emptied by robbers plus some standard-issue 'I see dead people' experiences, and you're away.

Or maybe it wasn't really Jesus on the cross after all, but someone who looked like him. Thinking Jesus was dead when he really wasn't would make the appearances possible. Add to that some confusion regarding the tomb, and you're heading toward an explanation that could account for both facts.

These are all *possible* explanations. They are the stuff of history: making hypotheses and testing them against the data. But as historical hypotheses, how good are they? Let's consider each idea in turn.

Take the swoon theory. How likely is it that Jesus wasn't dead? What are the chances that, after being up all night, after being subjected to horrendous beatings, after being mocked and taunted and deprived of food and drink, that after being nailed to a cross by professional Roman executioners, after having a spear thrust into his side producing a flow of water and blood—what are the chances that anyone would survive that? How likely is it that the people who buried him wouldn't have noticed that he was still breathing? And if he did survive all that, how likely is it that—in a cold dark tomb, without any medical attention—after 40 or so hours he would suddenly feel better again? How likely is it that he would have the strength to roll back the stone? And do you reckon his disciples, instead of saying, "Wow, you look rough" would conclude, "You look like a new creation"?

Or how likely is it that they simply went to the wrong tomb? Jesus' friends saw where he had been laid. And if they made an initial mistake, there was plenty of time to correct it.

And even if that was the case, when the disciples started declaring the resurrection, why didn't the Jewish or Roman authorities simply show everyone where the correct tomb was?

Or take the idea of a stolen body: who would want to steal it? How did the robbers get past the guards (Matt 27:62-66) and remove the large stone? Why did they decide to strip the body of its grave clothes and run it naked though the streets? If it was the authorities, why didn't they simply produce the body to prove the disciples wrong and stop the resurrection rumours? And if it was the disciples, why didn't they 'fess up—especially as, one by one, they were killed for their belief that Jesus had been raised?

What about the appearances? How likely is it that well over 500 people—people in different times and places, men and women, followers (like Mary), sceptics (like Thomas), and enemies (like Paul)—would all be subject to the same psychological phenomenon? And why, given the language and explanations that were available to them, did they all insist on using the language of 'resurrection' for what they were experiencing?

At this point, someone might point to Scottish philosopher David Hume's objection, namely: "No testimony is sufficient to establish a miracle, unless the testimony be of such a kind that its falsehood would be more miraculous than the fact which it endeavours to establish". A version of this claim is heard in discussions around contemporary atheism with the dictum 'Extraordinary claims demand extraordinary evidence'.

That *sounds* right, and as a general rule of thumb, it will serve you well in life. However, it smuggles in an assumption. Imagine for a moment that a miracle actually happened: why would you expect the evidence it left behind to be more than ordinary? A miracle, if it happened, would probably leave behind neither more nor less evidence than an ordinary event. And the same goes for testimony. If a miracle happened, and there were witnesses, there is no reason to assume that their testimony would be much different to the sort of testimony we expect for the non-miraculous. We need to ask, rather, what sort of evidence and testimony would we expect this sort of (miraculous) event to leave behind, and do we have that sort of evidence and testimony?

The Christian claim is that Jesus was raised from his tomb in his body. On the surface, this seems so unlikely as to be dismissed. Indeed, it did not immediately commend itself even to the first witnesses. However, once we carefully examine the actual evidence, the Christian claim starts to emerge like Australian speed skater Steve Bradbury in the 2002 Winter Olympics— strangely ahead, if only because everyone else fell over. There is simply no other explanation that works.

3. The force of the evidence

The New Testament writers provide an historical hypothesis for two historical data-points: that the tomb of Jesus was found empty, and that people saw him alive. The hypothesis is that he had been raised. And I think there are powerful reasons to take that seriously as the best possible way to account for the data in front of us. In fact, I would go so far as to contend that if any other (non-miraculous) event from this time in history had this kind of textual witness and explanatory power, it would be readily accepted. The rubbing point is not the evidence (which is just fine); it is the nature of the claim. For the claim involves... well, God.

You see, I think there is one very powerful argument against the resurrection of Jesus. It is an argument so powerful that it could sweep away everything else, including all sorts of excellent historical evidence: there is no God to do the resurrecting. And if there is no God to do it, then almost any other explanation will do.

But do you see, at this point we are no longer talking about evidence and historiography; we are talking about theology. We have been dragged, via historical reasoning, to the question of God. Which God? The kind of God who would raise Jesus from the dead.

Let me be clear: I do not think the historical evidence forces your hand. I do think it is good. It clears the ground for the claim that Jesus was raised, but I don't think it can push you over the line. Why? Well, I don't think the claim 'Jesus was raised from the dead' is the kind of thing that you assess, consider and accept on the basis of probabilities and then casually get on with your day. The claim that Jesus was raised from the dead is *self-involving*.

Actually, all knowledge is self-involving to some extent. We are not computers that merely process data without interest or subjectivity. As human knowers, we are subjects with interests, aims and intentions. We love, we resist, we invest and we recoil. In the act of knowing, there is the thing known, but there is also the 'I' doing that knowing. We are involved.

But there are degrees here. The knowledge that $2 + 2 = 4$, or that Tasmania is to the south of the Australian mainland, brings with it a different level of self-involvement than the knowledge that I have fallen in love with Susan. And where on that spectrum is the claim 'Jesus was raised from the dead'? The early witnesses put the self-involving nature of that claim in the front and centre of their witness: Jesus is raised from the dead, therefore change your mind and trust.

So—fair warning—let me just say it out loud: to receive the testimony that Jesus was raised from the dead would involve *you*, and would involve changes in *you*. It's not the sort of knowledge that can easily be accommodated into existing structures. It's an intrusive sort of guest, one that starts rearranging the furniture—and eventually (if you're not careful) you'll wake up one day and find it doing major structural work on the whole house.

Of course, I may be complicit in all of this. I may be deluded into receiving the testimony concerning Jesus for my own self-interested concerns to keep my job as a pastor, or to write this book, or to just not feel like a complete chump having wasted the better part of 38 years believing this stuff. Sure.

But that's true for you, too. You have your reasons for believing or not believing, and not all of them are disinterested. And we might as well just come out and say it—if this is true, if Jesus was raised by God, then it's true in a big, obtrusive, gaudy, self-involving way. If we are going to talk about God and hope and judgement and repentance and, oh, you know, the meaning of your life, there is more (but not less) going on here that just historical probabilities.

Chapter 4

FIRSTFRUITS! JESUS' RESURRECTION AND OUR OWN

'Death is a natural part of life.'
—Yoda, *Star Wars, Episode III: The Return of the Sith*

I GUESS I'M SOMEWHERE IN the middle of the bell curve when it comes to enthusiasm for new technology and software updates: enough of a technophile to be excited about the latest update, but not quite tuned into the mentality that has people sleeping overnight outside Apple Stores.

Being in the middle of that bell curve, I am part of that majority of people who are never quite across all the functions their smart phones can perform. I am therefore susceptible to surprises—sometimes inadvertently discovering that my phone can recommend a restaurant, remind me to pay a bill, or direct the flight path of a small commercial aircraft.

I think that for many Christians, what our faith has to say about the resurrection is like an underexplored smart phone. It sits there in our creeds and our Scriptures. We know it's there, we just don't know what we'd ever need it for in the trenches of day-to-day life. We know Jesus was raised from the dead. We just don't know how to connect that fact about Jesus with our own lives.

Which, as it happens, is the same mistake they were making at the church Paul planted in first-century Corinth.

First Corinthians 15 has already occupied our attention in the previous chapter, with its precious opening 11 verses on the resurrection of Jesus. These verses are remarkable for us, but they would have been very pedestrian for the church in Corinth. In my own day job as a preacher, I have a recurring nightmare that I might have misread the teaching roster and as a result be giving exactly the same sermon to the congregation I gave the week before. And if not whole sermons, I worry that I've given that story, that analogy, that anecdote a hundred times before. Paul similarly feels very self-conscious of the fact that *they've heard this from him before:*

> Now I would remind you, brothers, of the gospel I preached to you, which you received, in which you stand, [2] and by which you are being saved, if you hold fast to the word I preached to you—unless you believed in vain.
> [3] For I delivered to you as of first importance what I also received: that Christ died for our sins in

RAISED FOREVER

accordance with the Scriptures, [4] that he was buried, that he was raised on the third day in accordance with the Scriptures, [5] and that he appeared to Cephas, then to the twelve. [6] Then he appeared to more than five hundred brothers at one time, most of whom are still alive, though some have fallen asleep. [7] Then he appeared to James, then to all the apostles. [8] Last of all, as to one untimely born, he appeared also to me. [9] For I am the least of the apostles, unworthy to be called an apostle, because I persecuted the church of God. [10] But by the grace of God I am what I am, and his grace toward me was not in vain. On the contrary, I worked harder than any of them, though it was not I, but the grace of God that is with me. [11] Whether then it was I or they, so we preach and so you believed.

Notice how self-conscious Paul is of this all being old-hat to the Corinthians. I *remind you* (v. 1), I *delivered to you* (v. 3), so we preached and *so you believed* (v. 11). Everything Paul says here about the resurrection of Jesus is already in their random access memory. As the letter was first read, no-one would have been on the edge of their seat. On the contrary, just as someone raised in a good church can't help but start singing when they hit a part of the Bible familiar to them as a song, probably, as Paul was reading this, members of the congregation could almost 'sing' along. Even the form in which he was saying it was probably etched into their memories. This was the gospel *in which you stand* (v. 1).

I suspect that most Christians today are no different. Despite the predictable Easter newspaper article about some bishop somewhere who has his doubts about the whole thing, I think the average Christian in church is pretty across the idea that being a Christian entails the belief that Jesus was raised from the dead. I don't think we have a truth-in-advertising issue here—we're pretty up-front about this one. Getting upset because being a Christian involved believing *that* is a bit like getting upset because at a swimming pool party you got wet. There are some things you really should anticipate. (May I add that, for this reason, I'm not the biggest fan of Easter Sunday sermons that spend all their time proving the resurrection of Jesus actually happened. I don't come to church on Easter Sunday to be reminded of facts, but to be thrilled with hope.)

No, for the Corinthians their problem is exactly our problem: not a failure to believe the resurrection of Jesus, but a failure to connect what happened to him with what is happening (and will happen) to us. We, like them, are firm on the one and flaky on the other. "Jesus was raised from the dead. Absolutely! And that means that we will... um... hard to say, really. It's a bit of a grey area. Go to heaven when we die? Exist as eternal souls? Something about a 'rupture' or 'rapture' or something? Who knows?"

And Paul says that in light of verses 1-11, this kind of confusion makes *no sense*. It makes no sense to be firm on the resurrection of Jesus, and flaky on the resurrection of the dead:

Now if Christ is proclaimed as raised from the dead, how can some of you say that there is no resurrection of the dead? But if there is no resurrection of the dead, then not even Christ has been raised. (1 Cor 15:12-13)

The uncontested fact is the resurrection of Jesus, and the contested fact is the resurrection of the dead. And to hold the one and contest the other makes no sense. You can't believe that a thing is impossible in principle (the dead being raised) and true in reality (Jesus, a dead man, was raised).

In verses 13-19 Paul challenges their faulty logic with a rapid-fire series of statements. I'll list them out and insert the implied logic in italics (which are my words, not Paul's):

If there is no resurrection of the dead, then not even Christ has been raised—*but you do believe that Christ was raised.* (v. 13)

And if Christ has not been raised, then our preaching is in vain and your faith is in vain—*but you don't think our preaching and your faith is in vain.* (v. 14)

We are even found to be misrepresenting God, because we testified about God that he raised Christ—*and your whole faith rests on us telling the truth about God.* (v. 15)

And if Christ has not been raised, your faith is futile and you are still in your sins—*but you believe you are forgiven your sins.* (v. 17)

[*And if you are still in your sins,*] then those also who have fallen asleep in Christ have perished—*and you don't believe that.* (v. 18)

Somewhat obscurely, in verse 29 Paul points to a practice in Corinth of baptizing on behalf of the dead. It's not 100% clear what that means—I have a favoured theory I'm happy to share with you some time, but in some ways my guess is as good as yours.[34] What is clear, however, is that it is a practice (like making wedding vows when you intend to be faithless) that *somehow* affirms the very thing they are denying—that there is a resurrection of the dead.

Back in verse 19, Paul reaches a kind of climax:

> If in Christ we have hope in this life only, we are of all people most to be pitied.

Do you see what he is saying there? He's not just saying, "If Christ hasn't been raised, we're wrong and therefore to be pitied". No, he's saying that if the story of Jesus' resurrection is just a story of a remarkable thing God did once to one person, with no connection with our future, then that's a pitiable thing to stake a life on.

An Australian journalist was once interviewed about her faith and asked what she would do if it was somehow proven that Jesus Christ was never raised from the dead. She thought for a moment and said, "I think my faith would be strong enough to survive that". It may sound noble, but it is in fact nonsense. Paul is saying the exact

---

34 I am attracted to Thiselton's suggestion that some in Corinth, having witnessed the way Christians faced death, were led by the testimony of their deaths to receive baptism and follow Jesus: a baptism precipitated by the dying and now dead. See AC Thiselton, *1 Corinthians: A Shorter Exegetical and Pastoral Commentary*, Eerdmans: Grand Rapids, 2006, p. 275.

opposite—that Christian faith does not deserve to survive that. If you are a sceptic reading this book, and you come to the conclusion that Jesus was not raised, then please continue helping us Christians to see the light. Put some energy into it. Give us your best arguments. Don't patronise us with ideas that 'it gives them comfort' or 'it works for them'. Help us out of this mess. Our own Scriptures tell us that if we are wrong on this, we are a bunch of pitiable delusionals.

Positive consequences: 20-29

Paul thinks something is at stake here—something precious will be lost. But in verses 20-29 he turns to the positive: why the resurrection of the dead is essential to the Christian hope and eternity. Or, put more baldly, in verse 29 he tells us what the resurrection achieves.

I think as a rule we're much sharper on what the cross achieved than what the resurrection achieved. When it comes to the cross, Scripture gives us such wonderful, vivid explanations: a sacrifice in the temple, a price paid to release a slave from slavery, a ransom paid for a hostage, an exchange in a marketplace. Well, the good news is we have a vivid picture for what the resurrection achieves:

> But in fact Christ has been raised from the dead, the
> firstfruits of those who have fallen asleep. (v. 20)

Christ has been raised from the dead (= the historical fact), and this means that he is the firstfruits of those who have fallen asleep (= the theological meaning).

Picture it with me. You're a farmer looking out over your orchard in the very early days of spring. You see the firstfruits on the tree. Jesus' resurrection is like that.

What does it mean for Jesus to be the firstfruits? It means that Jesus is the best and that Jesus is the first. You see, in the Old Testament, the farmer gave his firstfruits to God because they were considered the best fruits. You didn't scratch around for the off-cuts. As an act of worship, you gave God your best.

The firstfruits were considered the best, but they were also, as everyone knew, the first *of the coming harvest*. For a farmer to give God his firstfruits was not just an act of worship; it was also an act of faith. Imagine for a moment that you are that farmer. No supermarkets, no refrigeration—just you, your farm, and a family to feed. Over the winter your supplies are slowly but surely going down, and by the end of the winter they are nearly all used up. Things get close to the line, but one day you wake up and the firstfruits are finally there to be eaten or taken to market. Wouldn't it be tempting to give that food to the family and then give God the next lot, once you have been looked after? By giving God the firstfruits, you're saying to your family: "There's more coming. We're giving this to God, and we'll trust him for the harvest."

Jesus: best and beginning

Now plug all that into the resurrection of Jesus. In his resurrection, Jesus is the best. He is the last Adam, the new man, the best of the crop to come. In his resurrection, he is God's new humanity *par excellence*—Humanity 2.0. He is humanity faithfully bearing God's image, humanity with all the sin and death and brokenness taken out of the system.

According to Psalm 8 (itself a reflection on Genesis 1 and 2), to bear the image of God is the vocation of every human being. It is an audacious plan: to put us, little old us, at the centre of the universe, the rulers of the works of God's hands. All things, says the Psalm, have been put under our feet (v. 6).

It is a state of affairs we don't see now. Well, at least we are doing an extremely ordinary job of it. But, says the writer of Hebrews, we see "him who for a little while was made lower than the angels, namely Jesus, crowned with glory and honour because of the suffering of death, so that by the grace of God he might taste death for everyone" (Heb 2:9).

Ruling over the creation is the general task of humanity, of 'Adam', but it was in a specific sense the task of the Messiah. In a world in rebellion against God, the Messiah, the son of David, was commissioned to put all his enemies under his feet.

And so, in his resurrection, Jesus fulfils Adam's role and David's role. In his resurrection, he becomes the True Human to whom God has given the rule of creation, and he becomes the True Messiah, the one commissioned by God to re-conquer a world in rebellion, and to defeat the last enemy: death.

He is the best, but he is also the beginning. He is the firstfruits *of the harvest to come*. That is, what God has done to and for Jesus, he will do for us. When you see the risen Jesus, you see our future. That's what the writer to the Hebrews is showing us: "At present, we do not yet see everything in subjection to him [that is, to humanity]. But we see him [that is, Jesus]..." (Heb 2:8-9). Notice the way these verses are so pregnant with hope. We do not *yet* see—but we will. And we know we will see humanity restored because we see Jesus, now raised and crowned with glory and honour.

This is similar to the point Paul makes back in 1 Corinthians. Do you see how he addresses their problems? The absurdity of the Corinthians' position is that it's like they look out at the orchard, they see the first peach appearing on the tree, and they say: "A peach. Great! I wonder what the rest of the fruit on that tree will be?" And Paul says: "You idiots, they'll be peaches! The peach reveals it to be a peach tree."

When we see the resurrection of Jesus and say, "A resurrection. Great! Now, I wonder what God will do with us?" Paul says: "You idiots, he's going to do with you the same thing he did with Jesus!" That's the point.

The resurrection of Jesus is the guarantee of our own. What happened to him will happen to those of us who are 'in him'. And just as the resurrection of Jesus secures our own, the whole creation itself waits for our resurrection so that it too can be liberated:

> For the creation waits with eager longing for the
> revealing of the sons of God. For the creation was
> subjected to futility, not willingly, but because of him
> who subjected it, in hope that the creation itself will
> be set free from its bondage to corruption and obtain
> the freedom of the glory of the children of God.
> (Rom 8:19-21)

Do you see? Because creation was designed to flourish under the rule of humanity, the creation now experiences our fall, our failure, as its bondage. It looks to the day when we will be revealed (that is, raised; see Romans 8:23), because once we have been raised in our bodies, creation will be free, because we will be restored as creation's vice-regents.

The end: 23-28

Back in 1 Corinthians, "firstfruits" is Paul's answer to the question, "How does the resurrection of Jesus relate to our future?" But as we see in verses 23-28, it is also the answer to questions about how Jesus changed the timetable.

For pagan people, like those we met in Athens and like those in Corinth, the big surprise is that there is a resurrection at all. But for Jewish people like Paul and the people we met in Jerusalem in Acts 2, the resurrection wasn't a surprise: that's what they hoped for—the resurrection of the dead. What was a surprise was the timing.

As we've seen, many Jews expected a resurrection of all people at the end of days. No-one expected a resurrection of one man in the present. And so much of the New Testament involved people having to rethink their eschatological timetable in the light of Jesus' resurrection. It looks something like this:

The two ages

The Resurrection of the dead

THE AGE TO COME

THIS AGE

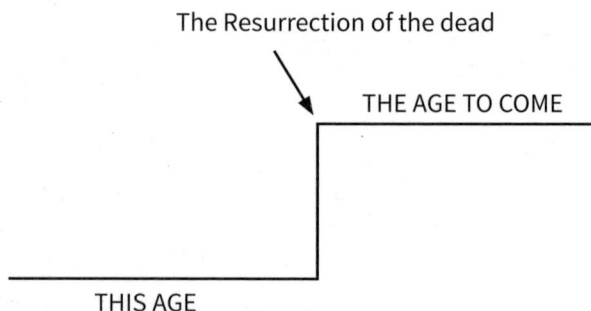

This diagram represents the Jewish sense that there were two ages: this present evil age, and the age to come, the time of God's kingdom. And the age to come involved, crucially, the resurrection of the dead.

The now-but-not-yet

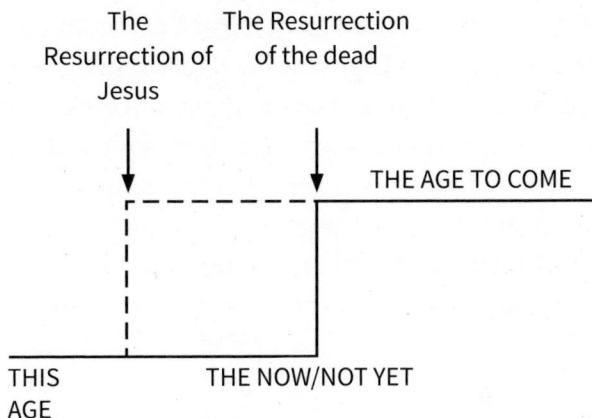

The Resurrection of Jesus

The Resurrection of the dead

THE AGE TO COME

THIS AGE

THE NOW/NOT YET

But in Jesus, the two tectonic plates—this age, and the age to come—crash into each other. And we now live not in the old age, where sin and death reigned, but neither in the new age when the last enemy (death) is defeated. We live in the overlap of the ages, in the now-but-not-yet. Not everyone has been raised; but someone has. And just as the resurrection of Aslan brought spring to the long winter of Narnia, so too the resurrection of Jesus has put into motion a process that cannot be reversed. Look how Paul puts it:

> But each in his own order: Christ the firstfruits, then at his coming those who belong to Christ. Then comes the end, when he delivers the kingdom to God the Father after destroying every rule and every authority and power. (vv. 23-24).

Do you see how the image of the fruitfruits helps us to get our heads around the change in the timetable? Faithful Israel was waiting for one giant harvest of resurrection at the end of time. But Jesus has been raised in the middle of history. He has had his turn, making him the firstfruits of the new age. As he was raised then, so it will be our turn at the end. The firstfruits signal the harvest to come. In the meantime, Jesus is getting on with the business of destroying all rule, authority and power that sets itself against God (v. 24)—also known as saving the world.

Resurrection lifestyle: 29-34

It is interesting that for Paul, one of the consequences of the Corinthians misunderstanding their future resurrection is sin: "Wake up from your drunken stupor, as is right, and do not go on sinning" (v. 34). We know from chapter 6 of this letter that the use of prostitutes by some of the church members was symptomatic of a lack of regard for what is done in the body—thinking of the body as an irrelevant piece of matter, rather than the very thing God would raise up on the last day: "God raised the Lord, and will also raise us up by his power" (1 Cor 6:14).

You see, to use the language of English theologian Oliver O'Donovan, the resurrection both *vindicates* and *transforms* the created order.[35] It vindicates it, because it is precisely

---

35 O O'Donovan, *Resurrection and Moral Order: An Outline for Evangelical Ethics,* Apollos, Leicester, 1986, pp. 70-1.

this creation that God is redeeming. He made it. It was a good call that God made when deciding to create the world. And he intends to redeem it—including (or especially) our bodies. Resurrection isn't God's move to Plan B, but God's determination to continue with Plan A.

However, the resurrection of Jesus also introduces genuinely new things. Singleness, for example, was not a highly valued vocation in the Old Testament. But in the wake of Jesus' resurrection, singleness (says O'Donovan) becomes cherished and valued precisely because it points us to the age to come, where Jesus says we will neither marry nor be given in marriage.[36]

So a practice like visiting prostitutes fails on both counts. It fails to testify to the goodness of marriage in the original creation; but at the same time, it fails to testify to the goodness of the age to come, believing that what we do in our bodies is morally irrelevant. Far from it! It is these very bodies that God intends to raise up (1 Cor 6:14).

Back in 1 Corinthians 15:34, Paul seems to have in mind a more general lifestyle shaped by a faulty eschatology. And the faulty eschatology can be summarized in the words of verse 32:

> If the dead are not raised, "Let us eat and drink, for tomorrow we die".

Notice the shape: life now, death then. It's a very common life pattern, perhaps the most common. Life now, death

---

36 O'Donovan, p. 70.

then; therefore grab what you can now. Death will come; death will eventually be the last word on every human life. Therefore, your best strategy is to grab what you can while you have the chance.

Death now, life then

But the resurrection of Jesus and the resurrection of the dead brings in a radically new possibility, a new pattern. Not life then death, but *death then life*.

Throughout his letters, we read of Paul willingly endangering himself, facing death and fighting temptation now. Why? It is because he's living the resurrection pattern of death now, life then. The thumping great secret at the heart of the universe is that in Jesus, the great reversal has begun—the firstfruits have appeared, and a world that looks like it's dying is about to spring out into radical new life. Investing a life in sin now is like investing your money in VHS video shops. Sin is an obsolete technology; it's so BC, so old school, so over.

Because of the resurrection, Christianity is, at its heart, a rebel's religion. The problem with the world is that it's far too conservative. It might look radical, but it is so deeply, deeply submissive. So horribly, embarrassingly wedded to the ancient regime of sin, death and Satan. It says to Death, "You win, sir. I understand that. And I don't mean to argue, or to appear insubordinate, but would it be okay if I played for a little first?" In *Star Wars Episode III*, when the Jedi Master Yoda says to Anakin,

"Death is a natural part of life", he speaks for many religious strategies beyond the Jedi world. It is extremely common for religions to work at helping people come to terms with death. To accept it. To call it natural. Even to learn to celebrate it.

But in the resurrection of Jesus, we don't say "You win". We say to Death, "You lose". We refuse the status quo; refuse to submit to death. We refuse to let the thug win.

At the time of writing this book, the 70-year commemoration services were happening in France for D-Day and the Battle of Normandy. This was the point in World War II when, on 6 June 1944, the Allies landed with an overwhelming show of strength in occupied France. It was the largest military operation ever undertaken, involving more than 150,000 troops, 5,000 ships and 11,000 airplanes. Although the actual victory of the Allies was not declared until May the following year, it is widely agreed that World War II was won at the Battle of Normandy. It was then that Europe was finally breached and the defeat of the Nazi regime was assured.

The resurrection of Jesus is like D-Day for sin and Satan and death itself. From here, the rest is a mopping-up campaign. Jesus' resurrection says to Death, "You've had your day. The game is up. The firstfruits are in the tree, the harvest is coming, and nothing you can do will stop it."

Chapter 5

INTERLUDE—WHAT HAPPENS WHEN WE DIE?

IN AROUND THE YEAR 150, Justin Martyr, the famous early Christian apologist, was defending the Christian faith in conversation with his Jewish friend Trypho. They were talking about what happens when you die and the differences between Jewish and Christian belief, and Justin said this to Trypho:

> For if you have fallen in with some who are called
> Christians, but who do not admit this... who say there
> is no resurrection of the dead, and that their souls
> when they die, are taken to heaven, do not imagine
> that they are Christians.

It's a measure of how far we have come (or how far we have fallen) that what Justin Martyr describes as a set of beliefs that are *not even Christian*, for us are almost the taken-for-granted Christian points of view: that we have souls, that they are immortal, and that they go to heaven when we die.

By contrast, we have been seeing that the Christian hope is not of immortal souls but resurrected bodies, a hope secured in the resurrection of Jesus. What does this mean for our other beliefs? When we say resurrected bodies, what exactly are we talking about? These bodies? New bodies? And if we are waiting for the resurrection, where are the dead now? And where does the traditional language of 'heaven' fit into all this?

In this chapter, we take a little interlude to address these issues. They come under three headings:

1. *How* are the dead raised?
2. Where are they *now*?
3. *Wow*—look at what happens to those who are still alive when Jesus returns!

How, Now, and Wow. (See what I did there?)

1. How?

If we are talking about resurrecting these bodies, how exactly is that going to happen? We know what happens to dead bodies—how on earth can we imagine they will be resurrected? Or is that even on the table? Are we given new bodies? Or spiritual bodies?

Fortunately for us, it is this very question that Paul addresses in 1 Corinthians 15:35:

But someone will ask, "How are the dead raised? With what kind of body do they come?"

In the context it is a cynical, scoffer's question. And Paul addresses it with a brilliantly simple but profound metaphor. He asks us to consider a seed:

> You foolish person! What you sow does not come to life unless it dies. And what you sow is not the body that is to be, but a bare kernel, perhaps of wheat or of some other grain. (vv. 36-37)

Think about the relationship between a seed and a plant for a moment. One is small, round and hard; the other is long, green and lush. If you were a new visitor to this planet, they might strike you as so different that a relationship between the two might not even occur to you. The transformation the seed undergoes as it becomes a plant is enormous.

So, too, the bodies of the resurrection will be transformed bodies. They will not be these bodies pulled out of their graves and dusted off to resume play. As Wright puts it, "A seed does not come to life by being dug up, brushed down and restored to its pristine seediness".[37]

Seeds and plants are unlike each other—but they are not unrelated to each other. They are not like football and beetroots, hump-backed whales and the Royal Post, oranges and life insurance—things from completely different spheres of life. On the contrary—amazingly,

---

37 Wright, *The Resurrection of the Son of God*, p. 342.

given the seeming differences, the plant and the seed are intimately connected. Indeed, *everything that the plant becomes was already inherent in the seed*. The plant is not the rejection of the seed—it is its fullness. When a seed becomes a plant, it is a fulfilment of the seed's ends and purpose.

So it is with the resurrection of our bodies, says Paul. The relationship with this body and that body is like *that*.

Paul goes on: "But God gives it a body as he has chosen, and to each kind of seed its own body" (v. 38). Each kind of body has its own glory or splendour. They do not compete with each other, but shine out as the glorious things they are. "It is no shame to a dog that it does not shine, or to a star that it does not bark."[38]

According to the creation account (which Paul probably has in mind as he writes this section of 1 Corinthians 15), in days 1-3 God created the light (day and night), the sky and the seas, and the land, and then in days 4-6 he filled those parts of creation with the bodies appropriate to them: animals for the land, birds for the sky, fish for the seas, and so on. And each kind of creature has its own kind of body—birds have one kind of flesh, animals have another, fish have another. There are bodies in the heavens—that is, the sky—and there are bodies on the earth.

What's Paul's point? "So it is with the resurrection of the dead" (v. 42). Just as our old bodies were made for the old creation, with a glory befitting the old creation, so

---

38 Wright, *The Resurrection of the Son of God*, p. 346.

too God will make new bodies fit for the new creation—bodies made perfect for the place they will be. Our old bodies are perishable, dishonoured, weak and natural; they will be raised imperishable, glorious, powerful and spiritual (vv. 42-45).

According to the Bible, there are two great bodies in history: the body of Adam and the body of Jesus. The one, Adam, the first man, was natural; the second, the last man, Jesus, was spiritual (v. 45).

'Spiritual' here is not being used in opposition to 'physical'. He means 'spiritual' as opposed to 'natural'. He's talking about the body's power source, not about its properties. It's like a train powered by steam and a train powered by electricity. A steam train is not made of steam, but run by it. And if a steam train is converted to electricity, what changes is not the constitution of its body but the source of its energy. (If you happen to be a trainspotter and that analogy doesn't work on some technical level, my humble apologies.) In the same way, our bodies are controlled by a natural power source in this creation, but in the new creation they will be powered by the Spirit of God. We who bear the image of the earthly man now will, at the resurrection, bear the image of the heavenly man then.

That's the first question: How?

2. Now?

Second, where are the dead in Christ now? To find an answer, we will go first to the main New Testament passage that directly addresses the issue, and then we'll sneak in on a few passages that don't directly address the issue, but which we might be able to raid from the side for some suggestive clues.

1 Thessalonians 4:13-18

The passage that addresses this issue most directly is 1 Thessalonians 4:13-18:

> But we do not want you to be uninformed, brothers, about those who are asleep, that you may not grieve as others do who have no hope. (v. 13)

The question, clearly, is the state of those who have died in Christ. Quite probably, it hadn't occurred to the Thessalonians that any of their loved ones would die before Christ returned. But since some have now died, they needed to swot up on the answer. For us, the answer is so obvious: they are in heaven—right? But that's not what Paul says:

> For since we believe that Jesus died and rose again, even so, through Jesus, God will bring with him those who have fallen asleep. (v. 14)

Do you see what he does? Where are the dead who died in Christ? How should we think of them? Answer: They have "fallen asleep" in him, and, at the resurrection,

RAISED FOREVER

God will bring all those people with Jesus. That is to say, they will be raised—which is confirmed in verse 16: "The dead in Christ will rise first". Now, they are asleep in him; then, they will be raised with him. Either way, Jesus has them.

Overwhelmingly, the language used by the New Testament to describe the Christian dead is that they are "asleep".[39] And it's not just that they are asleep, but that they are asleep "in the Lord". Why does the Bible use the language of sleep? Two reasons, I think: firstly, because "asleep" shapes how we are to relate to those who have died in Christ. What do you do with sleeping people? Well, you don't try to contact them. You don't talk to them, but neither do you worry about them. If you want to talk to them, you wait till they are awake. So, too, with us. Scripture forbids us from contacting the dead. Rather, we trust that they are in the care of God, that God will raise them up at the right time, and that we will be able to commune with them then.

But secondly, being asleep is the perfect picture for resurrection. Asleep, then awake. Horizontal, then vertical. The night, then the dawn. We sleep, we lay down, knowing that in the dawn we will rise.

---

39 In addition to 1 Thessalonians 4, see Matthew 27:52; John 11:11-12; Acts 7:60, Acts 13:36; 1 Corinthians 15:6, 18, 20; 1 Thessalonians 5:10; 2 Peter 3:4.

What about heaven?

Why doesn't Paul just say they are 'in heaven'? Well, surprisingly for us, the Bible rarely (if ever) uses 'heaven' in the way we use it. In the Bible, the word heaven/heavens almost always just means the skies. Heaven is also used derivatively to describe 'God's space'—the place where God is. So the Lord's Prayer addresses "Our Father in heaven" (as opposed to our fathers on earth).

Some verses that may at first sight appear to use 'heaven' in the way that is now so commonplace (i.e. to refer to our final home and hope) are, on closer inspection, doing something sightly different. The early verses of Colossians, for example, speak of "the hope laid up for you in heaven" (Col 1:5). But notice that here heaven is the place our hope is stored, not the object of our hope itself. The same sort of thing is going on in Matthew 6:19-20, where we are encouraged to lay up for ourselves "treasures in heaven". This is not because heaven is where we will go to collect them, but because heaven is where God is keeping them safe for us (see also 1 Peter 1:4). When the Gospel of Matthew uses the phrase "the kingdom of heaven" it is as a synonym for the kingdom of God ('heaven' standing for 'God' in the way 'the crown' stands for the Queen, or 'the turf' stands for the racing track). And, of course, the kingdom of God is the reign of God over his people. That's why in the Lord's Prayer we don't pray "Your people go" (to heaven) but "your kingdom come" (to earth). Sometimes our prayers are better theology than our theology.

But does the Bible ever use 'heaven' to mean 'the place where the dead in Christ go', or even 'our final home'? Well, not anywhere I can see. Because the truth is, the biblical hope is for a new heaven and a new earth. The biblical hope is that God will redeem this creation, not redeem us from this creation. It's not that we will be liberated from this world, but that this world itself will be liberated, as Paul tells us (see Romans 8:21).[40]

The idea that the dead are asleep has led some Christians to believe a doctrine called 'soul sleep'. This teaches that there is no consciousness at all for the dead between now and the resurrection of the dead. Tempting though this approach is, there are a few passages that on balance seem to rule it out for Christians. Chief among them is Philippians 1:20-24, where Paul says that to be away from the body (i.e. dead) is to be at home with the Lord. Paul says here that to be dead is "far better" (v. 23)— that "to live is Christ, and to die is gain" (v. 21). Surely, then, Paul envisions some sort of conscious enjoyment of Christ before the resurrection? Similarly, in 2 Corinthians 5, Paul expected to be away from the body but at home with the Lord. And Jesus tells the thief on the cross, "Today you will be with me in Paradise" (Luke 23:43).[41] Again, it would be surprising if that promise didn't imply some sort of conscious enjoyment of God at the point of death.

So, where are the dead in Christ now? They are asleep, they are at rest, and they are with God. Are they

---

40 More on this in the next chapter.
41 On where Jesus went when he died, see the discussion in the next chapter.

in heaven? Well, I guess Christ is at the right hand of the Father,[42] and the Father is in heaven, so okay. But it's not the language the Bible typically uses for the dead in Christ, and using this language carelessly today can import other things that we don't want to say. For example, when we habitually use the language of heaven for the final hope of those who die in Christ, we encourage a habit of mind that makes the resurrection of our bodies a kind of unnecessary addition to our hope, rather than the centrepiece of it.

Remember, Jesus says to the repentant thief on the cross, "Today you will be with me in Paradise". The dead in Christ are in a better place; but they are not yet in the best place. The better place is with Christ, but the best place is with Christ and his people in their bodies, in the new heavens and the new earth. If I can put it this way, the dead in Christ still hope along with us. They are waiting, like we are, for a better day—for the day of resurrection.

For my money, the sort of language we should use of the dead who have died in Christ is captured in Revelation 14:13:

> "Blessed are the dead who die in the Lord from now on." "Blessed indeed," says the Spirit, "that they may rest from their labours, for their deeds follow them!"

What is their situation now? It is blessed. Where are they now? They are "in the Lord". What is their experience

---

42 See Acts 2:33, 5:31, 7:55-56; Rom 8:34; Heb 10:12, 12:2; 1 Pet 3:22.

now? They are "at rest". Does the life they lived for Christ have any meaning? Yes, for their deeds will follow them. Beautiful.

3. Wow!

In 1 Corinthians 15:50-57, Paul predicts one more question: what happens to those who are alive at the coming of Jesus? If the dead are given resurrected bodies, well, that's all well and good for them. But what about those who are alive at the coming of the Lord? Do we, musical chairs-style, just get stuck in whatever body we had at the time of his coming?

> I tell you this, brothers: flesh and blood cannot inherit
> the kingdom of God, nor does the perishable inherit
> the imperishable. (v. 50)

Paul says that just as a body sown in the ground, a buried body, needs to be raised in power, so too the living—flesh and blood—cannot inherit the kingdom of God. That is, your body *as it is now* is not fit for the age to come. "Behold! I tell you a mystery. We shall not all sleep, but we shall all be changed" (v. 51). Not everyone will be dead at the coming of Christ, but everyone—dead or alive—will be transformed when he comes: "...we shall all be changed, in a moment, in the twinkling of an eye, at the last trumpet. For the trumpet will sound, and the dead will be raised imperishable, and we shall be changed" (vv. 51-52).

Conclusion

Back to the seed. CS Lewis once said that if you could see now what your neighbour will be then at the resurrection, you would be so taken with them that you would be sorely tempted to bow down and worship. We will be changed, and we will be glorious. However, we won't be beyond recognition. We won't look at each other then and say: "What?! I never knew you were...!?" No, we will look at each other then and say, I think, "Wow! Now *that* is what you were always supposed to be!" We will be most ourselves, most fulfilled, most who we were always meant to be, because then we will be like Jesus (1 John 3:2).

Chapter 6

THE RESURRECTION HOPE AND THE END OF THE WORLD

Life between the ages

In Israel my Rabbi kept getting asked by people, "What's going to be with the terrorism? What's going to be with the Palestinians? What's going to be with the process? What's it all going to be?"

One man was driving [my Rabbi] crazy with these questions day after day. And so he took him aside and said, "Look. We're Jews. As Jews we believe that *in the end* everything will work out. *In the end* there will be redemption. *In the end* there will be peace. *In the end* everything will be roses."

"Your problem", he said to the man, "is that you were born in the middle".

—Israeli journalist Herb Keinon
(in a speech to The Sydney Institute, 2008)

As we saw in chapter 4, the Christian life is lived between the ages. On the one hand, we don't simply live in the old evil age, but on the other hand, neither are we fully in the age to come.

We live in a strange time. Not everything that God has promised has come (the dead are still in their graves, the final judgement of evil is still to come, and there is a brand spanking new world waiting to be revealed). We are beset with problems, sins and sorrows. Our problem, as Herb Keinon's Rabbi put it, is that we live in the middle.

However, we live in a middle in which *something* has happened. A resurrection has happened. Indeed, *the* resurrection has happened—the resurrection of the Messiah, the Last Adam, the New Man, the firstfruits, the one whose own resurrection has triggered an unstoppable process that will culminate in the resurrection of our bodies, the judgement of evil, and the new creation. It is a process that cannot be stopped. Not by Satan. Not by death. Not by you. Or your sister. Not by anybody.

So here we are. Waiting. Longing. Living in hope. But living in a hope that (as the yoof say) is off the chain. Living in the now-but-not-yet. And in all of Scripture, there is no more poignant, beautiful or haunting meditation on this life between the ages than in Romans chapter 8. Paul frames our life in the present in these terms:

> The Spirit himself bears witness with our spirit that we are children of God, and if children, then heirs— heirs of God and fellow heirs with Christ, provided we suffer with him in order that we may also be glorified with him. (Rom 8:16-17)

Remember that pattern we saw in 1 Corinthians 15? That 'death now, life then' pattern? Well, this is another way of saying the same thing. Suffering now, glory then. We share in Christ's sufferings in order that we might also share in his glory. That is to say, the Christian life is hope-oriented. It looks to the future. It looks to a glorious future which, as Paul says, is of such a magnitude more glorious that it is "not worth comparing" with the present suffering (Rom 8:18).

Notice, by the way, how that future and glorious hope is described. The eager longing, the tilt forward, the great hope is for *what*? It is for "the revealing of the sons of God" (v. 19). That is, the great hope is for our resurrection, for our glorification, for what Paul goes on to describe as our "adoption as sons, the redemption of our bodies" (v. 23). That's interesting, because you might think that adoption as sons is something that is already ours. And it is—in one sense we have already been adopted (vv. 15-17; see also Eph 1:5). But in another sense, we await our adoption, our final inclusion in the family of God as brothers and sisters of Jesus; and that adoption process will be complete when our bodies have been redeemed and restored, just like our Older Brother's was in that graveyard in Jerusalem on the first Easter.

The redemption of our bodies is not just one of the cool things we get in Jesus, in the same way that there are all sorts of happy surprises in a good Show Bag. No, according to Romans 8, the redemption of our bodies is *the* hope in which we were saved (v. 24). The redemption of our bodies is not the icing on the cake; it is the hope toward which we strain and strive.

I mean, think of it: raised forever, in bodies fit for an eternity with God and his people. Broken bodies made whole, old bodies made new, sick bodies made well, weary bodies lifted up and made to run and jump and hug and sing. And because the great end-goal of the process of redemption in which we have been placed is still ahead of us, our lives are characterized by hope:

> For in this hope we were saved. Now hope that is seen is not hope. For who hopes for what he sees? But if we hope for what we do not see, we wait for it with patience. (vv. 24-25)

The Christian life is characterized by hope. But it is characterized by a particular kind of hope. It is not the hope of wishful thinking, the way a gambler might hope their horse wins, or a teenage boy might hope that girl notices him. Neither is it the kind of hope that is distant and far off: secure, but not close enough to impact me today. No, because of the resurrection of Jesus and the outpouring of the Spirit, the Christian hope is a hope that is already in motion. Someone has already pressed the 'go' button, and the whole thing is unstoppable, because Jesus has been raised from the dead. The first rays of the sun have already made their way over the horizon and broken through the darkness. It's like it's 24 December and it's almost midnight. It's like there is already a crack in the wall of the dam, and water is already gushing through it. It's like a virgin on the eve of the wedding day. Aslan is already off the stone table, and the long reign of winter has already begun to collapse. Spring in Narnia is now no longer something the inhabitants hope for in their future, but something that has invaded their present.

This hope is something you can take with you into the trenches of daily life. In any given week—at home, at the office, on the construction site, in the classroom— you will see signs of the old regime: sin and death and Satan doing their work as if they are still welcome. But they are not. How different to be able to look at sin in all its ugliness and be able to roll your eyes at it like your dad has just shown up in his 1978 disco suit. Sin is real, and it's horrible. But it's also tedious and boring, and it has officially been put on notice. Jesus has risen. Sin and death and the losers. The game's up.

That's why Christian hope—resurrection hope— is a particular kind of hope. It's intense. It's a weird mixture of excitement and frustration. Like a kid both enjoying and enduring the slow unfolding of an advent calendar. Like an overly long engagement. Like a fantastic meal the hungry guests at the table can smell, but not yet eat. The kind of hope, that is, that can make you groan with anticipation. And in Romans 8, everyone is in on the act. The whole creation, says Paul, "has been groaning together in the pains of childbirth until now" (v. 22). Why does the creation groan in this way? It's because it has a vested interest in our resurrection. It knows that when we are free, it will also be free. And we also join in the chorus of groaning with anticipation. Because we have the firstfruits of the Spirit, we "groan inwardly" (v. 23).

And, most surprisingly of all, the Spirit himself is helping to conduct the choir of groaning, as he "intercedes for us with groanings too deep for words" (v. 26).

We groan, but we groan toward a great goal. God is working all things together for good (v. 28). And what is that good? It is that Jesus should be "the firstborn among many brothers" (v. 29). God loves Jesus so, so much that he has placed him at the very centre of a band of brothers and sisters who will be conformed to his image, and who will share the rule of the universe with him. A band of brothers and sisters who will be raised and who will be like him. And God is presently at work in all things to make sure nothing hampers that goal.

The timetable for the end of the world

We are hoping for the appearing of Christ, the resurrection of our bodies, and the restoration of the universe. Can we get any more specific than that? I mean, in terms of a timetable. In terms of signs and programs and so on.

It seems to me that there are two tendencies amongst Christians at this point. On the one hand, there are those who are all too confident regarding what we can know about the future. Some people in this camp are able to produce elaborate charts, with future events pinned down to the very year or day. They claim to be able to reveal the true identities of the various beasts and dragons in the book of Revelation as contemporary world rulers.

On the other hand, there are people (sometimes in reaction to the first group) who declare their agnosticism on all things future. "Heaven or new earth? Resurrected bodies or eternal souls? Judgement or universal forgiveness: who knows? I guess it will just all pan out in the end."

The first approach is guilty of a wild over-confidence: never mind that the apostles regularly declare their ignorance on the details of God's future (1 John 3:2, Rom 8:24), or that Jesus himself knew not the day nor the hour (Mark 13:32), or that history is littered with false predictions and prophesies in this regard—but *we* know what Jesus and his apostles did not. Really? Lucky, I guess.

Yet the second approach is guilty of a strange ignorance on things that God has taken the trouble to reveal to us—some of which (such as the resurrection of believers) are hardly marginal issues in terms of the content of the gospel.

And so, with a healthy dose of fear and trepidation, let's consider what God has told us about the end. Aware that we are about to rush in where angels fear to tread and fools are as common as conversations on the weather in an English pub, let's get a lodestar to guide us. The Apostles' Creed, accepted by virtually all Christians everywhere, should help keep us from eccentricities here. It says that Jesus was...

...crucified, dead and buried.
He descended into hell.
On the third day he rose again from the dead,

He ascended into heaven and is seated at the right
   hand of the Father Almighty,
From where he will come again to judge the living and
   the dead.
I believe in... the resurrection of the body,
and the life everlasting.

Here, then, is a basic end-time program on which all Christians can agree:

1. Jesus is risen.
2. He is currently seated at the right hand of God the Father Almighty.
3. He will come again to judge the living and the dead.
4. The dead will be raised, and the new age will begin.

It is essentially the same timetable outlined in 1 Corinthians 15:23-28:

But each in his own order: Christ the firstfruits, then
at his coming those who belong to Christ. Then
comes the end, when he delivers the kingdom to
God the Father after destroying every rule and every
authority and power. For he must reign until he has
put all his enemies under his feet. The last enemy to
be destroyed is death. For "God has put all things in
subjection under his feet." But when it says, "all things
are put in subjection", it is plain that he is excepted
who put all things in subjection under him. When
all things are subjected to him, then the Son himself
will also be subjected to him who put all things in
subjection under him, that God may be all in all.

Notice the same basic pattern there?

1. Christ is raised (as the firstfruits).
2. He is now putting all his enemies under his feet (ruling from the right hand of the Father).
3. Then he will hand the kingdom to the Father so that God will be all in all.

The kind of eschatology reflected in the Apostles' Creed and 1 Corinthians 15 is Christianity 101. If you map out your future hopes on these sorts of statements, you won't go far wrong.

Too safe? Let's head out to a few more controversial topics.

Descended into hell?

If there was anything that raised a question for you in the Apostles' Creed, I'll bet it was the phrase "he descended into hell". *Did* Jesus descend into hell? And if so, what was he doing there?

The idea that Jesus descended into hell has a long history in Christian theology. In some periods and in some quarters the idea took on a life of its own, with paintings and stories of Jesus descending into hell to preach and to release the captives and so on. The idea of Jesus going into the Lake of Fire to do battle with Satan, like Anakin versus Obi-Wan in the climatic scene of *Star Wars Episode III*, is one that can be safely set aside as the product of pious imaginations rather than biblical testimony.

However, don't dismiss the Creed too quickly. In the New Testament, there are several words that refer to the fate of the dead. *Gehenna* is the one that most closely aligns with what we might mean by 'hell' as a place of final retribution. However, the word that comes across as 'hell' in the Creed is not a translation of the word *Gehenna*, but a word meaning 'the lowest regions', or 'the underworld', a concept more like *Hades*.[43] And Hades or 'the underworld' refers not to a place of final retribution but rather to the place where the dead now are, prior to their judgement.

So, what do we make of the Creed's claim that Jesus "descended into hell"? The first possibility—that Jesus went to the place of retribution, to 'hell'—lacks biblical warrant and isn't what the word means in the Creed. It can be safely put to one side.

The second possibility, suggested by none other than the great 16th-century reformer and theologian John Calvin, is that Jesus went to 'hell' on the cross. That is, on the cross, Jesus experienced 'hell'—the wrath of God for sin. Now, I'd think 'hell' is a pretty good description of what happened to Jesus on the cross, but it seems to me that it's unlikely that's what the writers of the Creed were referring to. No-one before Calvin thought they were, and chronologically it seems strange to go from 'suffered, crucified, dead, buried' and then jump back in time to say something more about 'crucified'.

---

43 The word 'hell' in the English version of the Creed was the Greek word *katôtata* and the Latin word *inferna*.

RAISED FOREVER

And so, I think the third and best option is that Jesus went into Hades. He was crucified, dead, and buried, and then he went to were dead people go. That makes sense. There are a number of places in the New Testament that could at least bear this meaning. Take, for example, Peter in Acts 2:

> "God raised him up, loosing the pangs of death,
> because it was not possible for him to be held by it.
> For David says concerning him...
>
> > 'For you will not abandon my soul to Hades,
> > or let your Holy One see corruption.'" (vv. 24-27)

Jesus *went* to Hades, but God did not *abandon* him to Hades. Instead, he raised him up from the pangs of death. Here it seems you have a pretty straightforward idea of Jesus dying, going into Hades and then coming back out again (see also Romans 10:6-7, Ephesians 4:9 and 1 Peter 3:18-20 for at least possible reference to the same idea).

Theologically, this idea has great potential to tie up a loose end. In the Old Testament, Sheol or Hades is a grim place, as we have seen. It's not the place of final punishment, but neither is it a place of blessing. But if Jesus descended to the dead, to Hades, and if there he brought blessing to those who died in the hope of God, then we have a way of understanding how the intermediate state, Hades, can now be described as "far better" (Phil 1:23) or "Paradise" (Luke 23:43). It's better because Jesus has been there. Jesus' victory extends there.

Do you need to be afraid of death? Do you need to fear

what happens between now and the resurrection? No! Jesus has made death a safe place for you. He won't lose track of you. Death, the last enemy, will be conquered in the end. But even now it has been tamed. At the name of Jesus, everything bows—things "in heaven and on earth *and under the earth*" (Phil 2:10). Even death and Hades. Jesus is Lord of it all.

The second coming

The Apostles' Creed also affirms that Jesus will come again to judge the living and the dead. The phrase 'second coming' doesn't actually appear in the New Testament, but we have repeated references to Jesus' coming, his return, his revealing. He is presently in heaven at the right hand of the Father, and he will be there "until the time for restoring all things..." (Acts 3:21). His work is yet to be completed. He is still yet to bring judgement (Acts 17:31) and salvation (Heb 9:28) to those who are waiting for him.

To the Thessalonians, concerned about their dead brothers and sisters in Christ, Paul comforts them with this detail:

> For since we believe that Jesus died and rose again, even so, through Jesus, God will bring with him those who have fallen asleep. For this we declare to you by a word from the Lord, that we who are alive, who are left until the coming of the Lord, will not precede those who have fallen asleep. For the Lord himself will descend from heaven with a cry of command, with

the voice of an archangel, and with the sound of the trumpet of God. And the dead in Christ will rise first. Then we who are alive, who are left, will be caught up together with them in the clouds to meet the Lord in the air, and so we will always be with the Lord. (1 Thess 4:14-17)

So, just filling in that timetable a little: Jesus will return, the dead in Christ will rise first, then those who are alive at his coming will be transformed, then the judgement, then the new creation.

The millennium?

Revelation 20 may at first (and even second and third) appear to complicate our rather simple timetable. There, the author speaks of a binding of Satan (v. 2), of a thousand-year reign of Christ (v. 4a), of a resurrection of (certain?) believers to reign with him at that time (v. 4b), and of a final defeat of Satan (vv. 7-10), before transmission returns to normal with the resurrection and the judgement (v. 11 and following).

What are we to make of this? Well, neither the scope of this book nor the courage of its author allow for detailed discussion or confident pronouncements. Three major options vie for our allegiance here:

- the *pre-millennial* position, which says that Christ's return will be *prior* to the thousand years
- the *post-millennial* position, which says that it will be *after* the thousand years

- the *amillennial* position, which argues that there is no literal thousand years, but the whole passage is simply using apocalyptic language for realities that we know from elsewhere in the New Testament—that Christ now reigns and will return to judge.

All three positions can make a good go of the details of Revelation 20, and all three are held by Jesus-loving, Bible-revering, God-honouring men and women. And all three come with certain baggage, both good and bad. I've felt the pull of the explanatory power of all three at different times. (In one particularly tumultuous week in which I was due to preach Revelation 20 on a Sunday, I think I was a-mil the week before, post-mil on Monday-Tuesday, and pre-mil for the rest of the week.) I *think* I'm amillennial in the end, but I certainly appreciate the urgency and sobriety of the pre-millennial[44] expectations of future tribulations, just as I appreciate the post-millennial optimism about God's ultimate ability to save the world.

As long as we can affirm together that Jesus is now Lord, that he will come again to judge the living and the dead, and that he will defeat Satan and bring salvation, I think we can keep working together.

---

44 Let me just add that there are two types of pre-millennial positions—the historic one and the more modern dispensationalist one that includes beliefs about a pre-tribulation rapture of believers and some exotic beliefs about the modern state of Israel, à la the *Left Behind* series. Just for the public record, I think that particular eschatology has a number of profound problems within it.

Heaven and New Creation

Okay, let's stand back for a moment and look at the big picture. Notice the shape of things with me. God made a good creation. It was subjected to frustration. It will be redeemed and liberated from its bondage to decay and brought into the glorious freedom of the children of God. This may be a good time to make explicit a few things that have already been suggested on the way through. I'll put it in a series of contrasts for the sake of clarity: not *this*, but *that*.

Not heaven, but a new creation

First, the Christian hope is not heaven but a new creation. Heaven may be where our hope is stored (1 Pet 1:4), but it is not the object of our hope. Our hope, rather, is in Jesus—and, through him, a new heaven and a new earth. As Oliver O'Donovan puts it, our hope is not to be liberated *from* creation; our hope is the liberation *of* creation. We do not long for redemption *from* our bodies, but for the redemption *of* our bodies.

Once you are alert to this, you see it everywhere. In the Lord's Prayer, we pray that God's kingdom would come and that his will be done "on earth as it is in heaven" (Matt 6:10). In the book of Revelation, we don't go up to the New Jerusalem; the New Jerusalem comes down to us (Rev 21:2). In Isaiah, it is a new heaven and earth that is promised (Isa 65:17), just as in 2 Peter we look forward to "new heavens and a new earth in which righteousness dwells" (2 Pet 3:13). "Our citizenship is in heaven, and from it we await a Saviour"—rather than waiting for a Saviour to take us there (Phil 3:20).

And when our Saviour comes, he will transform *our* lowly bodies to be like his glorious body (Phil 3:21). Just as there is continuity and discontinuity between our present bodies and our resurrected bodies, so too there will be continuity and discontinuity between this creation and the new creation. It will not just be this earth, tweaked a little bit and tidied up; but neither will it be an escape from this earth to an ethereal heaven. It will be *this* earth redeemed, *this* creation renewed, *this* universe liberated.

Not abolition, but fulfilment

Secondly, the Christian hope is therefore not abolition but fulfilment. Our hope is not that the creation will be destroyed, but that it will be made new—that its bondage to sin and decay will end, and that it will be brought into its glorious freedom and liberty. That is, our hope is that creation will become everything God always intended it to be—a universe under the rule of humanity, to the glory of God.

In the great vision of the new heavens and the new earth in Revelation 21-22, John describes the scene by saying that redeemed humans "will reign forever and ever" (Rev 22:5). Notice: *they* will reign. That is, *we* will reign!

Question: What will we be doing in the new creation? Answer: reigning. Why? Because redemption is not God's Plan B, his consolation prize. God's intention in creation was always to share his rule with his image bearers. Redemption is not God's way of saying, "Scrap that. Terrible idea. Never let them touch anything again." No, God's plan will be fulfilled—come sin, death, Satan, hell or high water, God will fulfil his purpose and share his reign with us, and we shall reign forever. The whole point of humanity from the beginning was to share God's rule (Gen 1:26). And the work of Messiah Jesus isn't just to snatch it back, but to reclaim the goal of a shared rule. We are invited to judge and to rule with Jesus (Dan 7:18; Matt 19:28; 1 Cor 6:2; Rev 22:5). He's really into sharing.

Not the end, but the beginning

Thirdly, the new creation is not the end but the beginning. The picture we have in Revelation 21-22 is not of everything wrapping up, of the curtain being drawn and the audience politely applauding the show. Rather, the resurrection of the dead and the new creation are just the beginning, the new birth of a new cosmos. It is the reality beautifully captured by CS Lewis in *The Last Battle*:

> And as He spoke, He no longer looked to them like a lion; but the things that began to happen after that were so great and beautiful that I cannot write them. And for us this is the end of all the stories, and we can most truly say that they all lived happily ever after. But for them it was only the beginning of the real story. All their life in this world and all their adventures in Narnia had only been the cover and the title page: now at last they were beginning Chapter One of the Great

Story which no-one on earth has read: which goes on
for ever: in which every chapter is better than the one
before.[45]

Not explanation, but vindication

Fourthly, in the Christian hope, we see not explanation
but vindication. The book of Revelation, written as it
was to persecuted and suffering people, is constantly
interacting with the problem of evil and suffering. Our
question in this regard tends to be "Why? Why does it
happen?" But the Bible's characteristic question (and
indeed the characteristic question of people in the middle
of extreme suffering) is not "Why?", but "How long?"

The final vision is not one of God getting out his
PowerPoint presentation to explain to us how all that
evil and suffering was really for the best. No, the final
vision is one of God wiping every tear from our eyes.
It's a vision of God healing the nations of all their war
wounds. Of beating every sword into a plough and every
spear into a gardening tool. Of providing consolation,
and making the promise: never again, never again.

Not us, but God

Finally, this Christian hope has one more feature worth
noting. And that is, it's not about us; it's about God.

---

45 CS Lewis, *The Complete Chronicles of Narnia*, book 7, *The Last Battle*,
    Collins, London, 1998, p. 767.

Throughout this vision, this picture, God and the Lamb are front and centre. The idea that heaven is you and me ignoring each other as we seek our own pleasure—that's not heaven, that's hell. Hell is where you finally get to live for yourself.

But in the new creation, God and Jesus are at the centre. To have any part of this new creation, you'd need to be cool with that. And that is pretty close to the heart of what it means to be a Christian—to be cool with the idea of God and Jesus being at the centre of the universe, and at the centre of your life and affections.

Responding to resurrection belief

Well, there it is. What do you do with this? All this continuity and discontinuity? All this now-but-not-yet? All the not-this-but-thats?

Paul ends his great resurrection chapter in 1 Corinthians 15 with a simple, profound and actionable statement. And the end of his *tour de force* on the shape of resurrection belief he says to the Corinthians:

> Therefore, my beloved brothers, be steadfast,
> immovable, always abounding in the work of the Lord,
> knowing that in the Lord your labour is not in vain.
> (1 Cor 15:58)

Paul says that the Corinthians are to be always abounding in *the work of the Lord*. The two risks here, I submit, are interpreting the phrase too narrowly or too broadly. It would be far too narrow, on the one hand, to assume the phrase means something like 'full-time, paid Christian ministry.' As Paul explicitly and patiently explained to the Corinthians back in chapter 7, the situation in which they were called is a perfectly good situation in which to live out their calling. "Always abounding in the work of the Lord" cannot mean "become a pastor or evangelist, or die trying".

On the other hand, it could be understood too broadly. Because the Bible's teaching on resurrection brings online a massive degree of continuity between this creation and the next (which it does), it could be tempting to assume that the "work of the Lord" refers to any work at all done in the Lord's name (which it doesn't). There is every reason to think that our cultures and our labours and our artifacts may be redeemed in the new creation (see Revelation 21-22). And that does bring a new dignity to our creative work in the present. But here in 1 Corinthians 15:58, when Paul uses the phrase "the work of the Lord", he is using it in a much more definite sense to refer to that sort of work that specifically promotes the gospel of Jesus.

Paul is not telling them to all become pastors or missionaries. But he is telling them, in the light of the resurrection, to pay particular attention and give particular energy to the work of the Lord—to those labours that are particularly directed at promoting the gospel (such as bearing witness at work, sharing the gospel with children in Sunday school, singing loudly at church, giving to missions, etc.).

Abound in *that* work. Or, as other translations of the Bible have it, give yourselves *fully* and *wholeheartedly* to those opportunities God has given you to help promote the gospel in your context and beyond.

There are probably pastors who need to hear this—pastors who are just going through the motions by not abounding in the work—just as there are many non-pastors who are living lives that joyfully abound in the work of the Lord.

Whatever your circumstances, go for it. Why? Well, because "in the Lord your labour is not in vain". Here is something that *will* (to quote Russell Crowe in *The Gladiator*) echo through eternity. Here is something that is not haunted by the possibility of just being a massive waste of time. Go for it! Give yourself fully to the work of the Lord. It is not in vain.

Chapter 7
THE RESURRECTION LIFE NOW

As an adolescent in church, I was aware that 'heaven' was a hard sell for our pastors and youth group leaders. They knew and we knew that the prospect of a future in heaven wasn't delivering the sort of life-changing hope we all knew it was supposed to. I distinctly remember observing two strategies being unleashed on us. The first (like the modified amplifiers for the hard rock band *Spinal Tap*) was to try and turn the volume up to 11. "Heaven is like your best, most pleasurable experience, times by infinity and extended for eternity."

The other was to turn up the guilt. "Heaven is like an endless church service, and if you don't love that then you don't love God enough."

Both, for me at least, failed. On the 'increase the

pleasure' strategy, I think there is something inescapably tedious and unfulfilling about the idea of a pleasant experience never ending. It sees us as mere pleasure-receptacles, rather than fully integrated human beings. The philosopher Robert Nozick once posed a thought experiment in which scientists have invented a pleasure machine able to stimulate a person's brain to give them the most pleasurable (and, as far as they can tell, real) experiences imaginable. And he asks: "Given the choice between the pleasure machine and real life, which would you choose?" Most people choose real life. Heaven seems to suffer a similar fate in my imagination.

At a more profoundly disturbing level, it starts to mess with your understanding of the Christian life and even the character of God. Taken to its extreme, it gives the impression that Christian obedience is a matter of being selfless now so that you can be selfish then. Life on earth becomes that brief moment of living for others, which can then be cashed in for an eternity focused on yourself. What kind of God presides over *that* kind of system?

Neither did the guilt strategy work. Despite being a good many kilometres closer to the truth that the unlimited pleasure strategy, it always carried with it an impossibly passive vision. It asks us to compare the riches of life lived as image bearers of God—lives of work and rest and play, of projects and puzzles and parties—and exchange that for Sitting In Church. Don't get me wrong. I love church as much as the next guy. But...

And buried within this vision was always the sense that 'heaven' was a kind of Plan B. Plan A (God sharing

RAISED FOREVER

his rule with his image bearers) didn't work, as we've all seen. And so Plan B (God retiring his vice-regents to heaven) was what the Creator did with people who had clearly proved to everyone that the whole share-my-rule-of-the-universe-with-my-image-bearers thing was never going to work. "This is why you can't have nice things."

However, I think once the nature of the resurrection hope is clarified, it starts to get exciting. For, as I trust we have seen, the Bible adopts neither of the strategies mentioned above. Rather, it holds before us the hope of a redeemed creation, centred around God and the Lamb, with humanity busy at work ruling the creation— building cities, making music, enriching communities to the praise and glory of God. That is something we could get excited about.

As I tried to demonstrate in chapter 6, it's worth clarifying what the Scriptures say about our hope, because it has a real impact on the present. It can help enormously as we face suffering in the present, and it gives a new and vital energy to our labour in the Lord, knowing that in the light of the new creation this labour is not in vain. We are not just shifting deckchairs on the Titanic. Resurrection hope makes a real difference in the present.

However, as we bring our journey to a close, I want to go one step further. For in addition to unlocking our imaginations, securing our future and fueling our hopes, the New Testament actually says that the resurrection of Jesus has ushered a new thing into our present: a new power, and a new experience. In fact, without giving an inch on the future-oriented nature of the Christian faith, the New Testament actually affirms that, in some sense, resurrection is an experience believers have already had. We have been "raised with Christ", says Paul (Col 3:1; see also Rom 6:4, Eph 2:6).

This line of thinking comes mainly in the book of Ephesians (with Colossians also cheering it on). In this great letter, Paul particularly applies the Christian gospel to the question of *power*: what does the death and resurrection of Jesus have to say to people lacking power? What sort of power does it offer? Look at what he says:

> I do not cease to give thanks for you, remembering you in my prayers, that the God of our Lord Jesus Christ, the Father of glory, may give you the Spirit of wisdom and of revelation in the knowledge of him, having the eyes of your hearts enlightened, that you may know what is the hope to which he has called you, what are the riches of his glorious inheritance in the saints, and what is the immeasurable greatness of his power toward us who believe, according to the working of his great might that he worked in Christ when he raised him from the dead and seated him at his right hand in the heavenly places, far above all rule and authority and power and dominion, and above every name that is named, not only in this age but also in the one to come. (Eph 1:16-21)

What you have here is a prayer. It is not a prayer that they will *have* something they don't have, but that they will *know* something and *see* something they already have. In particular, he wants the eyes of their hearts (a vivid if somewhat strange and slightly mixed metaphor) to see three things:

1. the hope to which God has called them (that is, the kind of thing discussed in the first six chapters of this book)
2. the riches of his glorious inheritance in the saints (that is, the rich bounty of being included in Israel)
3. the "immeasurable greatness of his power toward us who believe".

It's this third thing I'm interested in here. What is this 'great power' toward us who believe? We already have it (remember: the prayer is to *know* and *see* what we already have, not to *acquire* what we don't have), and it is immeasurable in its greatness. What is it?

Well, according to verses 19-20 it is "his incomparably great power for us who believe. *That power is the same as the mighty strength he exerted when he raised Christ from the dead"* (TNIV, emphasis added).

What power is at work in us? Well, the same power that raised Christ from the dead. That's what power is at work in us. And where do you see that? Well, you see it first of all in conversion. God didn't use one power to raise Christ from the dead and another power to see you converted. He used the same power both times (resurrection power apparently being a sustainable and reusable energy source).

Conversion as resurrection

Whether or not you are willing to ascribe the word 'resurrection' to the process of conversion depends very largely on what you think is going on when someone places their faith in Jesus. It depends on what state you believe Jesus has rescued them from. In verse 1 of chapter 2, Paul tells us exactly what state Jesus rescued us from: "You were dead" (Eph 2:1). Blunt enough for you?

You see, according to Paul, you and I were dead in our trespasses and sins. The key word there is 'dead'. Now, of course Paul isn't speaking of physical death. He goes on to parse out the experience of life outside of Christ, and it is very active stuff. He says that we once followed "the course of this world" and that we were signed up with the "prince of the power of the air" (v. 2), that we lived in "the passions of our flesh, carrying out the desires of the body and the mind" (v. 3). In short, we were captured by the World, the Flesh, and the Devil. And the shorthand for being captured by the World, the Flesh, and the Devil is, "You were dead". That, according to Paul, is what was wrong with us.

Nearly any worldview or religion or philosophy will have some account of what's wrong with us. In the Western tradition, many have argued that it is the structures of society that are to blame (that is, 'the World'). Marx, for example, saw the way capital is arranged by the few to exploit the many. Rousseau saw the social structures of society as retarding our natural freedom and innocence.

Others have located the problem in our desires and our nature (that is, 'the Flesh'). The Buddha, for example, argued that all suffering came not from the external world, but from our internal desires. Freud saw our problems as stemming from repressed and confused sexual ambitions.

And traditional religions often put a lot of stock in the spiritual realm, seeing the activity of demons and devils and spirits and the sources of our troubles (that is, 'the Devil').

When you search the Bible to work out the real nature of the problem, you find that it says, "all three". It acknowledges the way the structures of society so often bend our communities toward injustice, oppression and exploitation. It sees the brokenness of our internal world, the way our desires and our flesh are bent out of shape, away from God and from what is good. And it recognizes the reality of a spiritual realm, including a fallen and evil spiritual world.

That potent combination the Bible describes here in one phrase: "you were dead". Imagine a corpse in a coffin in a cemetery: the corpse is our flesh (dead to God), the coffin is the world (hemming us in), and the devil is the cemetery's grounds-keeper, in charge of the whole show.

"But apart from *that*, Mrs Lincoln, how was the play?"

The picture

Take a moment to feel the weight of this diagnosis. We're not sick; we're dead. We're not affected; we're enslaved. We're not constrained; we're trapped. It's probably the most comprehensive and brutal account of what's wrong that you could imagine.

Is there an upside? Well, one of the things about a diagnosis as serious as 'dead' is that it significantly reduces and focuses your treatment options. The diagnosis 'sick' could imply all sorts of things: drugs, changes in diet, exercise, rest, counselling, homoeopathy, acupuncture, meditation. So long as the diagnosis is sufficiently contestable and doesn't include the word 'dead', your treatment options are only as limited as your imagination and credulity. But once the diagnosis is 'dead', all those programs and options and courses of treatment fall silent. People who are dead aren't looking at treatment options. Actually, they aren't looking at anything. So the upside is that we know that if we really are dead, only one thing is going to help: we need a resurrection.

Down the road from where we live in Perth there is a suburb called 'Karrakatta'. Perth is one of those spacious Australian cities with a massive suburban sprawl. But Karrakatta is densely populated. Indeed, it is one of the most densely populated areas of Perth—with probably more people per square inch that anywhere else in the city. And yet no-one I know of has ever thought to plant a church there, run a mission there, put on an evangelistic concert there, or even begin a low-level, survey-based friendly door-knocking campaign to find out why people don't come to church.

Why? Well, Karrakatta is a cemetery. We already know why the residents of Karrakatta don't come to our churches. They are dead.

And what Paul is saying in Ephesians is that what is true of Karrakatta physically is true of every other suburb in our cities spiritually—the people in them are dead.

There is an important correlative of this severe biblical account of what our problem is. You see, when we Christians forget this diagnosis in our outreach— when we subtly replace 'dead' with 'very, very sick', 'really rough', 'on Struggle Street'—the risk is that we go in for shouting, or manipulation, or coercion.

A few years ago in Perth, there was a major event for young people. It was advertised on TV as a kind of motorcross slash hip-hop concert slash acrobatics show. As far as anyone could tell from the television, radio or paper advertising, the show wasn't Christian—it just promised to be a good time.

Given the way it was pitched, people were certainly surprised when, three-quarters of the way into the event, a bloke emerged and started preaching, culminating in a rather impassioned, shouty call for people to come down the front and give their lives to Jesus.

Why go in for that strategy? I don't know the organizers, but I reckon that somewhere pretty close to the heart of why a group of energetic, sincere and well-meaning Christians would take that approach is that they had lost track of the Bible's diagnosis. They had (I submit) forgotten that we are dead in our sins, and assumed we are just very heavily asleep and under-entertained.

Such events are an easy target, but they are just a large and gaudy version of what we often see, even in ministries of a more respectable theological pedigree. When a ministry starts to go in for coercion, heavy shepherding, control, or excessive reliance on technique or charisma or posture, we can be sure that part of what's driving it is a failure to see people as dead in their transgressions and sins.

What's the alternative? How does a proper understanding of the Bible's diagnosis help us to get this right? In 2 Corinthians 4, Paul says that he and his missionary colleagues have "renounced disgraceful, underhanded ways" (v. 2). It is only the God who said "let light shine out of darkness" (v. 6) who can shine his light into dark, dead hearts. That light is the light of the gospel (v. 4). Therefore, says Paul, his approach is "the open statement of the truth" (v. 2). That's the way the light shines.

Do you see the difference? Paul is under no illusions that applying the right kinds of pressure or using a bit of his own cunning is enough to get spiritually sick sinners over the line. Because he knows his target audience is dead, he is free to openly and honestly preach Jesus Christ as Lord (v. 5), trusting that God can (and does) use that message to bring light to the darkness and life to the dead.

The intervention

Dead people need a God who raises the dead—which is what the God and Father of Jesus specializes in doing:

> But God, being rich in mercy, because of the great love
> with which he loved us, even when we were dead in
> our trespasses. (Eph 2:4-5)

In Christian conversion, in someone coming to that point of putting their faith in Christ, God has been at work making the dead alive. The dead do not knock on the inside doors of their coffins. The dead do not participate in their own treatment, which is why the Bible can so emphatically and unreservedly describe the whole thing, the whole process of salvation, in one word: *grace*.

By *grace* you have been saved. (v. 8)

God reaches in. God makes the move. God does all the heavy lifting. God makes us alive. It is by grace we have been saved. God's part is to do the raising. Our sole contribution to our salvation is our deadness.

The verse goes on: not only have we been made alive, but we have also been raised up with Christ and seated with him in the heavenly places (vv. 5-6). The experience of conversion can be described in terms of resurrection not only because of the before-and-after shot (from death to life), but also because it is an actual participation in the resurrection of Jesus. By virtue of our union with Christ (because by faith we are included in him), we are now, spiritually, seated with him at the right hand of the Father. The resurrection of our bodies, which is future, is not just something we look forward to in hope, but a process that has already begun in us in spirit.

For some reading this, the language of 'dead, then alive' is actually a vivid experience of your conversion experience. Like the prodigal son of whom the father says, "My son was dead, and is alive again" (Luke 15:24), maybe your experience of the World, the Flesh and the Devil is quite easily captured in the word 'dead', and your experience of meeting Christ is equally well-captured with the words 'now alive'.

For others, not so much. Many Christians have been raised Christian and are not conscious of a time without Christ, whilst others of us have had bumbling, confusing journeys into the faith, such that any number of moments may or may not have been *the* moment it happened.

Never mind. The language belongs to us all, whether it captures your personal experience or not. Don't feel like you need to beef up your testimony, or go on a bender so that you can have the death-to-life narrative. If you are in Christ now, you have been made alive. Apart from the grace of God, you would be dead in your sins. That's all you need to know, really.

Living the resurrection life

"Awake, O sleeper,
and arise from the dead,
and Christ will shine on you." (Eph 5:14)

We see the power of resurrection in our conversion, and we also see it in the power to live a new life. We are God's "workmanship, created in Christ Jesus for good works, which God prepared beforehand, that we should walk in them" (Eph 2:10). We may not have been saved *by* good works, but we have certainly been saved *for* good works. Indeed, on this very day, God has already gone ahead of you to prepare in advance the good works in which you are to walk. (But, as a friend of mine said on Twitter recently, when you do come across those good works, try and act surprised.)

In the second half of Ephesians, chapters 4-6, Paul outlines the shape of a faithful life for people who have been raised with Christ. As a passage of Scripture, it repays careful attention, surveying as it does a vast range of human experience—church, personal relations, sexuality, music, marriage, family, workplace and spiritual warfare. The Bible's instructions for living a life faithful to God remind us that the Christian life is not intuitive. It is not that, having just walked out of our metaphorical coffins, God suddenly inserted computer chips into our brains with all the data and experience we need to live for God. Rather, Paul says that the Ephesians *learned* Christ. They:

> ...heard about him and were taught in him, as the truth is in Jesus, to put off your old self, which belongs to your former manner of life and is corrupt through deceitful desires, and to be renewed in the spirit of your minds, and to put on the new self, created after the likeness of God in true righteousness and holiness. (Eph 4:21-24)

The Christian life of obedience is like this: It is as if we have been brought out of our graves and made alive. Then, having been made alive, God says to us, "Take off your grave clothes and put on the clothes of the living". That is, put on your new self. To put on those new clothes is not a means of earning God's favour, as if by dressing in the clothes of the living long enough you'll eventually come alive yourself—the ultimate 'fake it till you make it' strategy. There's no need to fake it here. God has made you alive, therefore dress like you are alive.

What does that look like in the wild? Well, remember those good works God has already prepared for you to do today? Just do them. That's what you're all dressed up for.

Conversely, to return to sin is like deciding to dress in your old grave clothes again. To follow again the patterns of this world is like a living body deciding to lay on the ground and stay as still and as stiff as possible. Sure, it's physically possible to pretend your body is in a coffin. But you're not in a coffin. You are alive.

Paul uses precisely this sort of language in Colossians 3. There he talks through the process of putting off the old clothes and putting on the new. It's a process that involves our minds: "If then you have been raised with Christ, seek the things that are above, where Christ is seated at the right hand of God. Set your minds on things that are above..." (Col 3:1-2). Practically, this must involve pursuing the means by which the word of Christ can dwell in you richly (Col 3:16)—through singing, reading Scripture, getting in the way of good teaching, and so on.

It also involves no longer setting our minds on "things that are on earth" (v. 2b). That means putting off those things that ought to stay in the coffin—sexual immorality, impurity, evil desire, and so on (v. 5). And it involves putting on those things that belong to resurrected people—compassionate hearts, kindness, humility, and so on (v. 12).

It's a lifelong process, of course. Sometimes those new clothes feel awkward, strange, as if they belong to someone else. And sometimes those old clothes look comfy, well worn, nicely fitted. Don't buy it! Trust me—they really don't suit you any more. They make you look weird, old-fashioned, creepy, like you missed the memo, like you haven't been raised to life. But you have! Why live a coffin-shaped life? You have been raised with Christ. Live like it. Get out there in those new clothes, find those good deeds, and do them—and the same power that raised Christ from the grave is with you all the way.

Appendix
DISCUSSION GUIDE

THE QUESTIONS THAT FOLLOW are designed to help you discuss the content of *Raised Forever* with others—your spouse, your friends or the small group you meet with at church. Use these questions as a way of talking back over the content of each chapter and encouraging one another to put God's word into practice. Feel free to pick and choose your way through the questions, depending on how much time you have available.

Chapter 1: The strange hope—resurrection among the sceptics

1. In Athens, Paul noticed the city was full of idols. What do you notice about the spiritual realities of your own town or city?
2. Are there things in your own life that have taken the place of God? What are they? And how would you know?

3. What does Paul say the resurrection of Jesus gives proof of (Acts 17:31-32)? How does (or how should) that truth shape your life and your response to Jesus?

A prayer

Almighty God, who created all things and in whom all things live and move and have their being: so work in us that we would forsake all idols and serve only you, the true and living God, as we wait for your Son from heaven, Jesus Christ our Lord. Amen.

Chapter 2: The distant hope—resurrection and the story of Israel

1. How would you characterize the general Old Testament attitude to death?
2. When the hope of resurrection appears in the Old Testament (for example, in Daniel 12:2-3), what does it mean?
3. How does the story of Israel feed into resurrection belief?
4. According to Peter's speech in Acts, what does the resurrection of Jesus say about Jesus? What is the response Peter calls for, and why do you think he calls for that particular response?

A prayer

God of Abraham, Isaac and Jacob, you lifted up your people Israel when they were cast down, and you lifted up your Son from the grave as both Lord and Christ. Grant us repentance and faith, that we may know him as our Lord and trust him for our salvation. Through Jesus Christ our Lord, amen.

Chapter 3: The empty tomb

1. What were the general pagan and Jewish expectations about life after death? How do they affect our approach to the claims about the resurrection of Jesus?
2. What is the nature of the evidence we have for the resurrection of Jesus? What does Paul contribute? What do the Gospels contribute?
3. What do you make of the alternative explanations? Which are the stronger and weaker alternatives?
4. What does it mean to say that knowledge is 'self-involving'? And how does that affect our approach to the topic of the resurrection of Jesus?

A prayer

God and Father of our Lord Jesus Christ, who raised Jesus from the dead in our world and in our history: make us faithful in our testimony to the risen Christ, that the world may know your power and goodness. Through Jesus Christ our Lord, amen.

Chapter 4: Firstfruits! Jesus' resurrection and our own

1. What were the established traditions known and accepted by the church in Corinth (1 Cor 15:1-11)?
2. What implication have they failed to draw from what they have been taught (1 Cor 15:1-12)?
3. How would you explain the idea that Jesus in his resurrection is the 'firstfruits'?
4. What are some of the implications of living in the now-but-not-yet time between Jesus' resurrection and his return?

A prayer

God of all life, who in the resurrection of your Son has begun the defeat of Death: help us to live in the joyful hope of the resurrection of Jesus, the firstfruits of the harvest to come, so that our lives may point to the age to come. Through Jesus Christ our Lord, amen.

Chapter 5: Interlude—what happens when we die?

1. What is the relationship between this body and the bodies we will have in the resurrection? How does the seed-plant image help to understand it?
2. Where are the dead in Christ now? What is their experience?
3. What, according to Paul, will happen to those who are still alive at the coming of the Lord?
4. How could we change our language to better reflect the biblical hope?

A prayer

Almighty God, who keeps safe in your care all those who have fallen asleep in Christ: help us to face our own death and the deaths of our loved ones as those who have hope. Through Jesus Christ our Lord, amen.

Chapter 6: The resurrection hope and the end of the world

1. What is the nature of hope (Rom 8:24-25)?
2. How does the resurrection of Jesus shape the kind of hope we now have? How is our hope different from the hope of believers in the Old Testament?

3. What does it mean to say Jesus "descended into hell"? What comfort might that provide?
4. How would you describe the Christian hope to someone who was hearing it for the first time?

A prayer

Almighty God, who has promised to wipe every tear from our eyes and to make a new heaven and a new earth: help us to live with joy in the present, knowing that your final victory is assured. Through Jesus Christ our Lord, amen.

Chapter 7: The resurrection life now

1. What power is at work in us (Eph 1:19)?
2. Why did we need that kind of power (Eph 2:1)? What does it mean to be "dead"?
3. What are some of the things we are to put off? What things are we to put on?

A prayer

God our Father, who raised Jesus from the dead and who used that same power to raise us to new life in him: grant us the courage and joy this day to find the good works you have prepared for us, and to walk in them. Through Jesus Christ our Lord, amen.

Feedback on this resource

We really appreciate getting feedback about our resources—not just suggestions for how to improve them, but also positive feedback and ways they can be used. We especially love to hear that the resources may have helped someone in their Christian growth.

You can send feedback to us via the 'Feedback' menu in our online store, or write to us at info@matthiasmedia.com.au.